GARLAND STUDIES ON

ENTREPRENEURSHIP

edited by

STUART BRUCHEY
ALLAN NEVINS PROFESSOR EMERITUS
COLUMBIA UNIVERSITY

A GARLAND SERIES

RACIAL DISCRIMINATION AND MINORITY BUSINESS ENTERPRISE

EVIDENCE FROM THE 1990 CENSUS

JON S. WAINWRIGHT

GARLAND PUBLISHING, INC.
A MEMBER OF THE TAYLOR & FRANCIS GROUP
NEW YORK & LONDON / 2000

Published in 2000 by
Garland Publishing, Inc.
A member of the Taylor & Francis Group
29 West 35th Street
New York, NY 10001

10   9   8   7   6   5   4   3   2   1

Library of Congress Cataloging-in-Publication Data
Library of Congress Cataloging-in-Publication Data is available
from the Library of Congress.

Printed on acid-free, 250-year-life paper.
Manufactured in the United States of America

This book is dedicated to the memory of
Justice Harry Blackmun, Justice William Brennan,
and Justice Thurgood Marshall.

Contents

Preface

This book grew out of my involvement in assisting a number of state and local governments throughout the country in responding to the new rules for affirmative action first prescribed by the United States Supreme Court in late 1989. In early 1990, I was fortunate enough to be invited by former U.S. Secretary of Labor Ray Marshall and former Federal Reserve Board Governor Andrew Brimmer to participate in a study of minority businesses and business owners being conducted on behalf of the City of Atlanta and Fulton County, Georgia. As a result of my involvement in this very early study, I had the opportunity over the next several years to work on related studies in Texas, Florida, California, Missouri, Minnesota, and elsewhere. One thing I learned during the course of my involvement with these research studies was that blacks, Hispanics, and Native Americans appear to be more disadvantaged in business enterprise activity than in virtually any other aspect of economic life.

Yet, despite the large disparities in business enterprise activity that have been consistently documented by state and local governments throughout the country during the 1990s, plaintiffs challenging state and local affirmative action policies have routinely asserted that such findings are not indicative of discrimination. Plaintiffs, and their expert witnesses, are fond of suggesting that the data used to calculate minority business disparities are flawed, and even if the data are not flawed, that the disparities in evidence are meaningless because the data were not geographically or industrially disaggregated enough. Similarly, they speculate that other factors besides discrimination might be responsible for the observed disparities. There is much more rhetoric than economics in these speculations. Never is any data presented showing that non-discriminatory factors can adequately account for the observed disparity. Instead contrived hypothetical examples are presented to persuade the judge that it is possible that this *could* happen.

Well, many things are possible, but not all are equally probable. Given the tremendous size of the racial and ethnic disparities I have observed over almost a decade of research, it seems to me very disingenuous for plaintiffs, plaintiffs' experts, and in some cases state and federal judges, to suggest that race and ethnicity plays no significant role in explaining the present day disadvantaged status of minority businesses in the United States. This book grew out of an effort to satisfy myself that the disparities facing minority business enterprises in this country are not as easily explained away as some would have us believe.

This book would never have been written without the generous support and encouragement I have received over the years from Ray Marshall of the University of Texas at Austin. I am also deeply indebted to Jorge Anchondo, Andrew Brimmer, Mario DePillis, David Evans, Mark Grayson, Colette Holt, Cheryl McVay, and Brian Trinque for their comments, criticism, and encouragement in the course of conducting my research. All remaining errors are mine alone.

I want to express my deepest thanks to my family—my wife Paddy, my parents Dave and Carol, and my children Katy, David, and Amy—for their steadfast encouragement and unflagging faith.

Jon S. Wainwright
Austin, Texas
1999

Tables and Figures

CHAPTER 1

Economists in the Courtroom

In contrast to wage and salary workers, the issue of racial and ethnic discrimination among self-employed business owners has received little attention from economists. As Aronson (1991, ix) observes:

> Self-employment is unquestionably the oldest way by which individuals offer and sell their labor in a market economy. At an earlier time, it was also the primary way. Despite this history, its principal features and the characteristics that differentiate self-employment from wage and salary employment have attracted the attention of only a handful of students of the labor market.

Recent changes in the law, however, have made the continued constitutionality of affirmative action in public sector contracting and procurement contingent upon documenting the existence of racial and ethnic disparities in self-employment and business enterprise, quantifying their magnitudes, and identifying whether they indicate the presence of economic discrimination within narrow geographic, industrial, and racial or ethnic boundaries. Given the extensive economic literature on racial discrimination in other contexts, particularly wage and salary employment, economists seem well suited to assist in making such assessments. This study is devoted, in small part, to this task.

INSTITUTIONAL AND NEOCLASSICAL THEORIES
OF ECONOMIC DISCRIMINATION

Labor economists have been influencing law and public policy on matters of discrimination for almost sixty years. Although many economists mark the beginning of the profession's involvement in matters of racial discrimination with the publication of Gary Becker's ([1957] 1971) now classic *The Economics of Discrimination*, it began much earlier. Gunnar Myrdal's *An American Dilemma: The Negro Problem and Modern Democracy*, published in 1944, impacted an entire generation of social scientists, jurists, and policy makers (Myrdal [1944] 1962). It remains unparalleled in the scope and depth with which it examined "the Negro problem" in the United States in the years leading up to World War II. That same year, the publication of Herbert Northrup's Harvard Ph.D. thesis (Northrup [1994] 1971) was the first of several detailed professional inquiries that were to arise into employment discrimination against minorities, particularly blacks, in the South and within trade unions (*e.g.* Ginzberg 1956; Marshall 1965, 1967).

These early institutionalist investigations are important because they combined political, psychological, sociological, and economic theory with historical perspective, case studies, and quantitative data to better understand what discrimination is, how it arises, and how it can be changed. As such, these studies were enormously relevant and useful to public policy and the law. *An American Dilemma* and *Organized Labor and the Negro* were both cited extensively by the U.S. Supreme Court in the 1954 *Brown vs. Board of Education I* (74 S.Ct. 686) and 1955 *Brown vs. Board of Education II* (75 S.Ct. 753) decisions. Similarly, the work of Northrup, Ginzberg, and Marshall played an important role in bringing about fundamental changes in trade union practices towards minorities.

Institutionalists have been critical of Becker's theory of employment discrimination,[1] arguing that the abstractions necessary to conduct the analysis within the confines of price theory and competitive equilibrium render it essentially useless for purposes of informing public policy. Marshall (1974), for example, is a proponent of this view. According to Marshall and Christian (1978, 220–27):

> Explicit and implicit definitions of discrimination used in a theory or conceptual framework have important implications for policies to combat discrimination. Becker [1957], Arrow [1972a; 1972b], and Welch [1967] consider discrimination to be based on attitudes or preju-

dices which cause people to want to avoid associating with or hiring particular individuals. Thus Becker and Arrow speak of a "taste for discrimination" for which maximizing agents are willing to pay. Moreover, in Becker's theory whites are concerned about physical distance from blacks and are willing to pay a premium not to associate with them.

We have found the neoclassical definition and formulation of discrimination to have very limited value either in understanding the employment disadvantages of blacks or in prescribing policies to eliminate them. We have also found it important to distinguish [institutional discrimination], from the specific, overt discriminatory actions of particular decision makers. We have therefore found *behavior* models (which look at the behavioral characteristics of employers, unions, white workers, black workers, government agencies, and their interactions with each other and the environment within which they operate) to be more useful than the narrow formulations of the neoclassical model. . . .

Thus, employer discrimination is better understood in a social rather than an isolated individual context. Although isolated economic tendencies, as outlined in neoclassical models, define *theoretical* tendencies drawn from restrictive assumptions, they are not necessarily predictive of *actual* behavior, because economic tendencies can be counteracted by social forces. In making employment decisions which maximize profits, employers must therefore consider the reactions of customers, unions, present employees, government agencies, black organizations, and the public, all of which can influence costs, revenues, and the ability to operate. . . .

The neoclassical model is therefore likely to produce misleading policy conclusions, principally because it exaggerates the importance of market forces in overcoming discrimination. We agree that market forces tend to eliminate racial discrimination but think that this tendency may never change employment patterns because it is counteracted by important forces not included in the neoclassical model. . . .

Our main argument, then, is that discrimination does not necessarily result from the attitudes of individual decision makers. As a result, we think public policy should be directed toward changing the context within which people operate as well as toward changing their attitudes and tastes. Consequently, we are more interested in determining what kinds of changes need to be done to improve black employment opportunities than we are in the highly technical and difficult analytical task of isolating the impact of racial prejudice on black employment patterns. We think institutional discrimination is so pervasive that it influences such productivity factors as education, on-the-job training, and skills training, making it difficult to pinpoint these factors in the total constellation of forces determining black employment patterns. [Marshall and Christian's italics]

In the traditional view, discrimination is everywhere and always an individual and essentially overt phenomenon. In the institutionalist view, in contrast, discriminatory actions and prejudices also—and more importantly—filter through the institutions of the labor market.[2] Under both theories, however, one important way in which discrimination manifests itself is as quantitative differences in earnings or occupational attainment that cannot be accounted for by differences in productive ability.

ECONOMISTS IN THE COURTROOM

In contrast to theory, far less controversy exists regarding the usefulness of the statistical and econometric methods developed by Thurow (1969), Ashenfelter (1972), Oaxaca (1973), Blinder (1973), and others, for determining whether or not economic discrimination exists at all—as opposed to how it arises or how it changes. These quantitative methods recognize that due to human capital investment (*e.g.* Willis 1986), compensating differentials (*e.g.* Rosen 1986), or sectoral assignment problems (*e.g.* Sattinger 1993), racial wage differentials can still arise between groups even in the absence of discrimination.

Essentially, these empirical procedures attempt to control statistically for differences in the endowments of human and financial capital ("qualifications" or "productivity") between minority and non-minority groups and individuals. The proportion of an observed disparity that remains unexplained after such qualifications are accounted for is attributed to racial and ethnic differences in the market mechanisms that generate employment opportunities and incomes ("discrimination"). To the extent that the differences in qualifications and productivity across races are themselves not attributable to labor market discrimination, these adjusted, or net, differentials provide better measures of discrimination than the unadjusted, or gross, differentials that don't account for such differences. Oaxaca and Ransom (1994) detail the current state of the art regarding the empirical techniques for estimating such adjusted differentials.

The broader acceptance among economists in all camps of these empirical techniques—in contrast to competing theoretical approaches—is no doubt because determining whether or not economic discrimination exists is a far more straightforward problem than determining why discrimination arises or how it can be changed. For present purposes I restrict myself to the former exercise, recognizing that, while necessary, in and of itself such an exercise is certainly not sufficient to yield answers to the questions that most interest observers like Marshall and Christian. As I have mentioned, however, a series of recent decisions by the U.S. Supreme Court requiring public agencies to produce quantitative evidence of discrimination prior to pursuing race-conscious affirmative action policies has given renewed importance and relevance to this kind of exercise.

This type of economic empiricism concerning the relationship between discrimination and racial disparities in earnings *among wage and salary workers* has played an important role in U.S. courts during the last twenty-five years. According to Ashenfelter and Oaxaca (1987, 321):

> Although [Becker's] *The Economics of Discrimination* has left a large scholarly legacy, we believe the empirical methods associated with the study of race and sex discrimination . . . have had a far larger impact on how Title VII of the 1964 Civil Rights Act is enforced than is commonly understood by economists.

The quantitative decomposition of observed racial and ethnic differentials into "qualifications" and "discrimination" components has slowly gained acceptance in U.S. courts as a viable form of evidence of employment discrimination. This trend began in the early 1970s. Examples of early cases include *United States v. U.S. Steel* (371 F.Supp. 1045, N.D. Ala.) in 1973, *Wade v. Mississippi Cooperative Extension Service* (528 F.2d 508, 5th Cir.) in 1974, and *Kyriazi v. Western Electric Company* (476 F.Supp. 335, D. N.J.) in 1979. In many of the early cases, although regression techniques were utilized in discovery, the published opinions contained little or no discussion of the use of such techniques. Several later cases explicitly addressed the use of regression analyses and began delineating the conditions under which such analyses would be deemed relevant. Important cases in this regard include the Supreme Court's 1973 decision in *Casteñeda v. Partida* (51 L.Ed.2d 498), the U.S. District Court decision in *Vuyanavich v. Republic National Bank* (505 F.Supp. 224, N.D. Tex.), and the Supreme Court's 1986 decision in *Bazemore v. Friday* (92 L.Ed.2d 315).[3]

This trend is due in part to the considerable practical advantages that the statistical definition of discrimination possesses compared to the jurist's traditional definition. Connolly, Petersen, and Connolly (1996, A–89) observe that:

> Multiple regression analysis is a device for making precise and quantitative estimates of different factors on some variable (or variables) of interest. The practical use of multiple regression analysis has grown markedly over the past twenty-five years, due to the development of statistical methodology itself, increasing availability of statistical data and most importantly, the development of the computer. The premise which supports the use of multiple regression analysis in Title VII cases is that skill factors are relevant determinants of decisions made in hiring, promotion, compensation, firing and other aspects of employment. The separation of the impact of an employer's unlawful discrimination from the impact of decisions based on valid job-related skill differences is at the heart of employment discrimination cases and is the point multiple regression seeks to demonstrate.

When evaluating discrimination empirically, the economist looks for evidence of "disparate impact" while the jurist looks for evidence of "disparate treatment." According to Ashenfelter and Oaxaca (1987, 322):

> Although . . . definitions of market discrimination have become almost commonplace to an economist, to lawyers they are irrelevant and hopelessly complex. For the legal mind, discrimination is above all an action taken by someone to the disadvantage of someone else because of their race. . . . Classic examples of such actions are the maintenance of separate racial lines of progression in a paper products factory, the refusal to hire women for certain blue-collar jobs, or the maintenance of separate pay scales for black and white workers in similar jobs. These are all examples of *disparate treatment.*
>
> It is not hard to see that the appearance of disparate treatment is easy for an employer to eliminate without making any change in behavior at all. Differential hiring or pay scales may be supported by simply asserting that all hiring and pay is determined by employee supervisors. Who is to say whether employee supervisors *really* use "merit" in making their decisions? This obvious difficulty has lead the courts to recognize that some actions may be discriminatory because

they have a *disparate impact* on the employment or compensation of one or more protected race . . . groups.

To most economists the insistence on finding "smoking gun" evidence of discriminatory actions, motivation, or intent seems quite irrelevant to determining whether market discrimination exists.[4] In crude terms, for economists evidence of discrimination merely requires the presence of "unexplained" differences in compensation or employment. In practice, the economists' view has made considerable headway in the courts. [Ashenfelter's and Oaxaca's italics]

The move towards judicial acceptance of statistical definitions of discrimination has been accompanied by advances in empirical techniques on the part of labor economists (Cain 1986; Neuman and Silber 1994) and improvements in available labor market data on the part of the federal government (Hamermesh 1990; Stafford 1986). This trend has contributed substantially to the growing influence of economists in the courtroom as well as to the development of a substantial empirical literature on employment and wage discrimination.

PUBLIC SECTOR AFFIRMATIVE ACTION FOR MINORITY BUSINESS ENTERPRISES

Recently, the Supreme Court has applied many of the same legal doctrines to business discrimination cases as they have to cases of discrimination in employment or education. Indeed, two of the principal precedent cases cited in the landmark 1989 *City of Richmond v. J.A. Croson Co.* (109 S.Ct. 706) decision, discussed below, were the 1978 *University of California Regents v. Bakke* (98 S.Ct. 2733) (a higher education case) and the 1986 *Wygant v. Jackson Board of Education* (106 S.Ct. 1842) (an employment case). This linkage relies on the belief that questions about the existence of discrimination against minority business enterprises can be evaluated by adapting the empirical techniques developed by labor economists for the evaluation of the presence of employment discrimination to situations of self-employment and business ownership.

Virtually all the economic investigations of employment and pay discrimination to date, however, have focused on *paid employees*, rather than the *self-employed*. In fact, the self-employed typically are excluded from such studies so as not to confound the results for paid workers.[5]

This is surprising since racial and ethnic disparities tend to be even larger in business enterprise and self-employment than in other areas of economic life. In 1990, for example, blacks represented roughly twelve percent of the U.S. population, eleven percent of the civilian labor force, and ten percent of total employment. However, blacks received less than eight percent of total money income, held under three percent of the nation's wealth, owned only three percent of the nation's businesses, and made only one percent of business sales. A similar pattern is evident for Hispanics, as well as for other racial and ethnic minorities, with the exception of certain ethnic Asian groups. Hispanics in 1990, for example, were nine percent of the population, but less than eight percent of the civilian labor force and total employment. They received only about five percent of total money income, held less than two percent of the nation's wealth, owned only about three percent of U.S. businesses, and accounted for only about one percent of all business sales (Bureau of the Census 1992b, various tables).

In tandem with growing minority political power and in response to emerging evidence that minorities were more disadvantaged in business enterprise than in almost any other aspect of economic life (Coles 1969; Brimmer 1966; Brimmer and Terrell 1971; Cross 1971), a substantial number of public sector affirmative action programs emerged between 1969 and 1989 aimed at promoting the participation of self-employed minorities in public contracting and purchasing activities.[6] These minority business enterprise (MBE) programs originated at the federal level and spread gradually throughout the 1970s and 1980s until they were present in a large number of states and municipalities throughout the country. By 1989, more than thirty-five states and almost two hundred local governments had passed some sort of affirmative action initiative for MBEs (Council of State Community Development Agencies 1993; MBELDEF 1988; Benjamin 1990, 65).

A primary purpose of these MBE programs has been to mitigate the alleged disadvantaged nature of minority business enterprise by formally encouraging their participation in government purchasing processes. Several types of initiatives have emerged. Some operate on the demand side of the market and some on the supply side. On the demand side, four types of programs have arisen to increase the amount of business governments do with minority-owned firms: contract set-asides, good-faith effort subcontractor goals, bid preferences, and subcontractor compensation clauses. Governments have also attempted to influence the supply side of the market through various initiatives to improve the prospects of minority-owned firms for winning government business, such as providing financial assistance and technical assistance to prospective minority bidders, conducting extensive outreach efforts to bring more minority firms into existing procurement and contracting networks, and operating certification programs to minimize the potential for non-minorities to abuse MBE programs by establishing minority "fronts."

Because of MBE programs, the public sector has come to represent a significant source of demand for the goods and services of minority and female entrepreneurs. The federal government, for example, purchased about $203 billion in goods and services in fiscal year 1995. Of this, about $11.2 billion (5.5 percent) was spent with minority-owned firms, and $3.6 billion (1.8 percent) with women-owned firms (U.S. Small Business Administration 1996, 325). The state and local sector, which spends an estimated $250 billion each year (Enchautegui, et al. 1996, i–ii) on goods and services, is also an important source of demand for minority-owned and women-owned firms. The State of Texas, for example, has a program for purchasing from such firms, as do the Cities of Austin, Houston, Dallas, Fort Worth, San Antonio, and others. Overall, the State of Texas spent about $5.8 billion on procurement in the 1996 fiscal year, of which $936 million (16.1 percent) was spent with minority-owned or women-owned firms (General Services Commission 1996, sec. IV). Similar procurement initiatives are in place in many other state and local governments throughout the country.

CONSTITUTIONAL CONTROVERSIES OVER AFFIRMATIVE ACTION FOR MINORITY BUSINESS ENTERPRISES

Like affirmative action policies in employment and education, these MBE policies have been controversial. For example, a major trade association for the construction industry, the Associated General Contractors of America, has been pursuing legal challenges to MBE programs since before *Croson* was handed down (La Noue 1994a, 63–66). Some observers believe that, fundamentally, these controversies reflect differences in economic and status motives between majority and minority groups in the United States. Martin Luther King, Jr., for example, observed that "[h]istory is the long and tragic story of the fact that privileged groups seldom give up their privileges voluntarily" (King 1963). Successful business enterprises can confer considerable economic, social, and political power on their owners (Marshall 1991b). Non-Hispanic white males have more or less monopolized opportunities in the business sector since the founding of the nation (Washington 1907, 40; Jones 1971, 8), and that status is perceived to be threatened by the expansion of public policies intended to promote minority or female business ownership.

In part, however, controversy also exists because the rationale for affirmative action is not well understood by the public or by most policy makers (Marshall 1991b). Much of the controversy has taken place in court. The federal courts have a tortuous history in dealing with affirmative action. Since the 1970s, they have wrestled with the question of whether affirmative action was a constitutionally permissible government activity under the equal protection clause of the Fourteenth Amendment, or whether it was "discrimination in reverse." A number of important affirmative action cases made it all the way to the U.S. Supreme Court during the 1970s and 1980s, yet in none of these was a majority of justices able to agree on the most important issues.[7] However, a position did emerge on the court that " . . . advocates the use of strict scrutiny [the strictest level of judicial review available] for equal protection analysis of all affirmative action cases. This position was first advanced by Justice Powell in the now famous *Bakke* decision and gained considerable momentum during the mid-to-late 1980s." (Fitch 1992, 568).

This position finally predominated in the landmark U.S. Supreme Court decision in *City of Richmond v. J.A. Croson Co.*, which constitutionally legitimized the concept of "reverse" discrimination by adopting the "strict scrutiny" standard for the first time with respect to state and local government affirmative action. In 1995, *Adarand Constructors, Inc. v. Peña* (115 S.Ct. 2097) overturned the 1980 *Fullilove v. Klutznick* (100 S.Ct. 2758) decision upholding federal affirmative action and extended strict scrutiny to the federal government as well. The heightened evidential and procedural requirements imposed by the majority in *Croson* have restricted greatly the ability of states and their political subdivisions to promote the development of MBEs.[8]

Strict scrutiny is the most stringent standard of review available to the Court. Under strict scrutiny, when state or local legislation involves a racial classification, whether it is blatantly invidious (as with the notorious Jim Crow Laws) or purportedly benign (as with affirmative action initiatives) the presumption of constitutionality usually afforded legislation by a state or its subdivisions is reversed. To establish a racial classification as benign, a state or local government must conduct detailed fact-finding regarding the presence and extent of racial discrimination in a particular geographic region and industry sector in order to demonstrate its "compelling interest" in legislating a racial classification. Finally, if a compelling interest is established, any legislation implemented in response to that interest must be "narrowly tailored" so that its scope is limited to remedying such identified discrimination. It must represent "a precise response to the problem, and must not impair basic liberties by its overbreadth" (Ducat 1978, 201).[9]

Croson concerned a challenge to the City of Richmond's affirmative action program for contracting with minority-owned businesses. That program required that 30% of city construction contract dollars be subcontracted to minority-owned businesses. Richmond claimed, among other things, that the huge disparity between the small percentage of city contracting dollars going to blacks (0.67 percent) and the large percentage of blacks in Richmond's general population (50 percent) justified setting aside a portion of city contracting business for minority-owned firms. The city argued that this disparity, coupled with other evidence that was introduced, supported its inference of racial discrimination (*Croson* at 714, 725–26).

A majority of the Supreme Court disagreed, ruling that Richmond's evidentiary basis was insufficient to support its MBE program (Cohen 1989). The Court held instead that affirmative action for minorities is constitutional only if accompanied by a strong body of quantitative and qualitative evidence documenting the existence, scope, and causes of racial disparities among the relevant populations of minorities to whom a particular affirmative action program is intended to apply—something the City of Richmond did not possess.

All of Richmond's evidence was dismissed by the majority as unacceptable: "None of these findings, singly or together, provide the city of Richmond with a 'strong basis in evidence for its conclusions that remedial action was necessary'" (*Croson* at 724, citing *Wygant*). The Court ruled that Richmond's statistical comparison overstated the magnitude of the racial disparity involved and thus did not provide conclusive evidence as to the size, *or possibly even the existence,* of a racial disparity. Since construction contractors possess characteristics not generally found in the overall general population, the Court declared, it was inappropriate to make comparisons to the general population in attempting to establish the existence of a racial disparity in public contracting and procurement spending. Drawing on statistical precedents established previously in employment discrimination litigation (*e.g.* Rigelhaupt 1976), the Court ruled that:

"[W]hen special qualifications are required . . . comparisons to the general population (rather than to the smaller group of individuals who possess the necessary qualifications) may have little probative value." [quoting *Hazelwood School District v. United States*, 433 U.S. 299 (1977)] . . .

In the employment context, we have recognized that for certain entry level positions requiring minimal training, statistical comparisons of the racial composition of the [general] population may be probative of a pattern of discrimination. . . . But where special qualifications are necessary, the relevant statistical pool for purposes of demonstrating discriminatory exclusion must be the number of minorities qualified to undertake the particular task (*Croson* at 725).

By using the share of minorities in Richmond's general population as the reference group for its disparity index, the city erroneously included any minorities that, as a matter of personal preference, would never have participated in the public or private sector construction business—even in the complete absence of racial discrimination. This has the effect of artificially inflating the denominator of the disparity index, causing its overall value to drop. Due to this downward bias—the majority reasoned—it was impossible, in the absence of additional information, to determine what the actual magnitude of the disparity was, or, for that matter, whether it really existed at all. The majority did not appear troubled by the fact that the denominator would have had to drop from fifty percent to less than one percent in order for the disparity to be eliminated.

After declaring Richmond's measure invalid, the Court pronounced the formulation of a measure it considered to be the correct benchmark in such a case. The appropriate reference group, according to the Court, should be the percentage of MBEs in the *business* population of an area, not the percentage of minorities in the *general* population. The former is the same group being measured in the numerator of the index and, the majority reasoned, it is therefore the most appropriate benchmark.

In the process of invalidating the particular forms of evidence in Richmond's case, the Supreme Court did, however, reaffirm that "proper" statistical evidence—evidence that revealed significant racial disparities between a government's minority procurement and the availability of minority businesses in the surrounding economy—would be an acceptable form of evidence in future affirmative action litigation. Such evidence—possibly standing alone, or in combination with other factual showings—could be used to support an inference of discriminatory exclusion. According to Justice Sandra Day O'Connor, the author of the majority opinion: "There is no doubt that '[w]here gross statistical disparities can be shown, they alone in a proper case may constitute prima facie evidence of a pattern or practice of discrimination' under Title VII" (*Croson* at 725, quoting *Hazelwood*). Justice O'Connor cited favorably a 1983 statistical study used by the State of Ohio to support its minority purchasing initiatives (*Croson* at 725). In *Ohio Contractors v. Keip* (713 F.2d 167, 6th Cir.) the state based the denominator in its disparity index on the percentage of the state's businesses that were minority-owned. Specifically, they documented that ". . . minority businesses constituted 7% of all Ohio businesses but received less than 0.5% of state purchase contracts" (*Keip* at 171).[10]

Four of five Justices in the *Croson* majority also acknowledged that state and local governments had a constitutional duty not to contribute to the perpetuation of racial discrimination in the private sector of the local economy. They argued that as long as it is identified "with the particularity required by the Fourteenth Amendment," states and local areas have the right to "use [their] spending powers to remedy private discrimination . . ." (*Croson* at 720). Therefore,

if the city could show that it had become a "passive participant" in a system of racial exclusion practiced by elements of the local construction industry, we think it clear that the city could take affirmative steps to dismantle such a system. It is beyond dispute that any public entity, state or federal, has a compelling interest in assuring that public dollars, drawn from the tax contributions of all citizens, do not serve to finance the evil of private prejudice (*ibid.*).

The Supreme Court ruled that there was no evidence of this sort in the record in Richmond's case.

For these and other reasons, the majority in *Croson* concluded that "[t]here was no direct evidence of race discrimination on the part of the city in letting contracts or any evidence that the city's prime contractors had discriminated against minority-owned subcontractors" (*Croson* at 714). The dissenting Justices argued in response that racial discrimination in Richmond was and is so pervasive—and knowledge of it so obvious—that the city council could appropriately conclude that racial discrimination was a problem without undertaking extensive prior fact-finding. Consider the remarks of Justice Harry Blackmun:

I never thought that I would live to see the day when the city of Richmond, Virginia, the cradle of the Old Confederacy, sought on its own, within a narrow confine, to lessen the stark impact of persistent discrimination. But Richmond, to its great credit, acted. Yet this Court, the supposed bastion of equality, strikes down Richmond's efforts as though discrimination had never existed or was not demonstrated in this particular litigation. . . .

So the Court today regresses. I am confident, however, that, given time, it one day will do its best to fulfill the great promises of the Constitution's Preamble and of the guarantees embodied in the Bill of Rights—a fulfillment that would make this Nation very special (*Croson* at 757).

Even conceding Justice Blackmun's point—which the *Croson* majority did not—it is still possible, following Justice Powell's line of reasoning in *Bakke*, to argue that substantial fact-finding is nevertheless a prudent prerequisite to implementing affirmative action since it serves other important purposes in addition to establishing the presence of discrimination. These purposes include: (1) building consensus in the community regarding the need for and fairness of affirmative measures (*Fullilove* at 2789 fn.8; *Croson* at 730; Marshall 1991b, 16); (2) defining the scope of the injuries suffered by minority businesses (*Croson* at 727); (3) serving to identify the necessary remedy (*ibid.*); (4) providing numerical benchmarks for assessing the progress of initiatives; and (5) establishing "logical stopping points" to ensure that initiatives are not "ageless in their reach into the past, and timeless in their ability to affect the future" (*Croson* at 723, quoting *Wygant*).

It is important to point out, however, that the type of disparity index used in *Ohio Contractors v. Keip* no doubt has bias problems of its own. By limiting the scope of allowable statistical comparisons to the outstanding population of minority-owned businesses in a given industry, the Court effectively excludes from judicial consideration any and all firms which have either left or never entered the industry due to racial discrimination. This exclusion is conceptually similar to the way in which official unemployment figures ignore "discouraged workers"— workers who left or never entered the labor force for lack of opportunity—and thereby understate the "true" extent of unemployment (Marshall and Briggs 1989, 119–120).

The type of index that has been endorsed by the Supreme Court may therefore systematically *underestimate* the racial disparity in an area since it excludes by definition those businesses against which racial discrimination has perhaps been most effective—those actually driven out of business by racial discrimination and those potential entrepreneurs who, because of discrimination, never had an opportunity to enter certain lines of business at all. Such disparity indices are thus inherently conservative measures of the extent of disparity. If disparity indices such as these indicate the presence of discrimination, the evidence ought to be all the more convincing.

No further attempt is made here to weigh the relative merits of either the minority or the majority points of view in this respect. It is the majority's argument, however, not the minority's, that carries weight in the lower courts. Therefore, in affirmative action jurisprudence, statistical evidence matters—but it must be properly assembled.

THE AFTERMATH OF *CROSON* AND *ADARAND*

Rather than stipulate that the history of racial discrimination in the United States has compressed available business opportunities for minorities, the *Croson* and *Adarand* decisions have made proving that discrimination against minority businesses and their owners even *exists* a necessary first step in establishing the constitutionality of minority affirmative action in public contracting. In the nine years since *Croson* was handed down, dozens of state and local MBE programs have been challenged in both state and federal courts on grounds that they did not possess such proof. Some programs have been permanently enjoined as a result, including, for example, programs in Atlanta, Philadelphia, Houston, Miami, and Columbus, Ohio.

Many agencies and jurisdictions have voluntarily suspended their MBE programs, and a number of legislative bodies have already or are considering the termination of some or all public sector affirmative action within their jurisdictions.[11] Others have chosen to defend their MBE initiatives, and have commissioned research studies in an attempt to meet the rigorous new legal standard. Since *Croson* was decided in 1989, at least 75 so-called "disparity" studies have been commissioned by various state and local governments throughout the nation (La Noue 1994b, 536–40; Enchautegui, et al. 1996, 1; MBELDEF 1991).[12] Their purpose has been to determine the existence of compelling interest by determining whether or not discrimination against minority businesses is evident in the industries and geographic markets covered by a particular affirmative action program. Some studies were commissioned in response to legal challenges, others in order to ward them off.[13] With the *Adarand* decision, many more studies and many more legal challenges can be expected (VanMiddlesworth 1995, 28).

All of these disparity studies have attempted to document the *gross* differences between the percentage of minority owned businesses in an area and the percentage of public and private sector sales and receipts that they earn. These gross statistical disparities, when they are found to exist, are often buttressed with anecdotal accounts of overt discrimination from individual minority business owners and historical evidence of discrimination in the region.

Although I do not read *Croson* or *Adarand* as requiring it, there is language in the majority opinion that could be read to suggest that—despite Justice O'Connor's reaffirmation of *Hazelwood*—in addition to documenting gross disparities, defendant governments might also be required to show that these disparities cannot be attributed to factors other than discrimination. In discussing whether Richmond's evidence of extremely low membership in the local construction contractors association has any probative value, Justice O'Connor writes (*Croson* at 726),

> standing alone, this evidence is not probative of any discrimination in the local construction industry. There are numerous [possible] explanations for this dearth of minority participation, including past societal discrimination in education and economic opportunities as well as both black and white career and entrepreneurial choices.

Most disparity studies have documented extremely large gross disparities between minority and non-minority businesses. Only a few, however, have conducted formal economic tests for discrimination that attempt to evaluate racial disparities in business enterprise while holding some or all of these other influential factors constant (*e.g.* NERA 1994; Lunn and Perry 1993). This is partly due to the paucity of statistical data on business enterprise in general, and on minority business enterprise, in particular.[14] Evans and Leighton (1989, 519), for example, note that:

> [w]hile recent studies have enhanced our empirical knowledge of the role of small businesses in the economy, data limitations have forced these studies to sidestep a number of issues that are basic to an economic understanding of firm formation, dissolution, and growth.

These data problems are particularly acute with respect to minority-owned business enterprise (Bendick 1990, 96; Handy 1989, 65; Wainwright 1991, 35–73).[15]

In large part, the present study is an attempt to see what can be done with the best available data to formally test for the presence of discrimination against minority business owners, and so address Justice O'Connor's criticisms.

RACIAL AND ETHNIC DISPARITIES IN BUSINESS ENTERPRISE

Disparities in Self-Employment Rates and Earnings

In light of their controversial nature—strict scrutiny notwithstanding—it is particularly important that public sector minority business development programs are understood to be fair and in the public interest. Marshall (1991b, 19–20) observes:

> As Justice Powell noted in his concurrence in *Fullilove*, which upheld the federal minority set-aside program, "[R]espect for the law, especially in an area as sensitive as this, depends in large measure on the public's perception of fairness. It therefore is important that the legislative record supporting race-conscious remedies contain evidence that satisfies fair minded people that [governmental] action is just."

Although clearly not yet the case in U.S. courts, among the few economists who have examined the issue, there is unanimous agreement that large and apparently persistent racial and ethnic disparities exist in self-employment rates and incomes in the United States. These disparities have been noted by a number of scholars, including Moore (1983), Borjas (1986), Borjas and Bronars (1989), Meyer (1990), Aronson (1991), Silvestri (1991), DeVine (1994), Fairlie and Meyer (1996) and Fairlie (1996). Aronson's (1991, 77–78) recent monograph on self-employment concludes, for example, ". . . the self-employment rate remains relatively low . . . among minority groups. . . . [Further,] [t]he earnings of the self-employed are generally much lower than those of their native white counterparts. . . ."[16]

An early study by Borjas (1986, 487), for example, estimated self-employment rates by race and ethnicity among the native-born and among immigrants using sample microdata from the 1980 decennial census. Borjas concluded that in both groups, non-Hispanic whites generally had the highest self-employment rates while blacks and Hispanics had the lowest.[17]

Meyer (1990, 6–7), using a combination of 1980 census data and 1982 *Characteristics of Business Owners* data, corroborates these findings, concluding that:

> [b]lacks, other minorities and women all tend to have lower self-employment rates than white males. . . . The black self-employment rate for males of 4.3 percent is less than one-third that of whites which is 13.3 percent. The number for black women is also about one-third the figure for white women. Those of Spanish origin have self-employment rates about one-half the white rate. . . .

More recently, Fairlie and Meyer (1996, 764–66) estimated self-employment rates for a wide variety of racial and ethnic groups using sample microdata from the 1990 census. Their estimated nationwide black male self-employment rate for 1990 of 4.4 percent was, again, about one-third of the estimated non-Hispanic white male rate of 13.4 percent. The figure for black women was estimated to be 2.0 percent, less than one-third of the rate of 7.3 percent for non-Hispanic white women. Fairlie and Meyer conclude (761–762):

> There are also large differences within broad ethnic and racial groups. All of the European groups have self-employment rates near or above the [overall] U.S. rates for men and women. . . .
> The self-employment rates of men and women in Hispanic ethnic/racial groups are typically below the average U.S. rates. . . .
> Overall, black ethnic/racial groups have the lowest self-employment rates of any broad group.

Other recent studies of self-employment rates that include findings by race and ethnicity are DeVine (1994, 23) and Silvestri (1991). Both draw on the *Current Population Surveys* for their data. DeVine reports findings for both 1975 and 1990. Silvestri reports data from 1983 and 1990. Both sets of findings document large racial and ethnic disparities in self-employment rates consistent with those reported above.

In addition to disparities in self-employment rates, the earnings of minority business owners are substantially lower than that of their white male counterparts. Moore (1983, 498) for example, using data from the

1978 *Current Population Surveys*, estimated that average annual earnings of black males in nonagricultural self-employment in 1977 were only 69 percent that of corresponding white male earnings.[18]

Borjas (1986, 487) estimated average annual earnings of self-employed black males in 1979 to be only 63 percent that of self-employed white male earnings among the native-born and 66 percent among immigrants. He also reported large disparities for both immigrant and native-born self-employed Hispanics of Mexican origin. Somewhat smaller disparities were recorded for Hispanic Cubans and other Hispanics. No disparities were observed for self-employed Asians.

Borjas and Bronars (1989, 594) estimated that the weekly earnings of self-employed non-Hispanic black males in 1979 were less than 63 percent of non-Hispanic white male earnings while those of Hispanic males were about 75 percent of non-Hispanic white male earnings.[19]

I have estimated self-employment earnings for men in 1989 using a sub-sample of 1990 census microdata.[20] Table 1.1 shows that the earnings disparities documented in the 1980 data by Borjas, Meyer, and others have apparently persisted into the 1990s and have, if anything, worsened. The average annual earnings of self-employed blacks, for example, are only 59.3 percent as high as the earnings of self-employed

Table 1.1. Estimated average annual earnings of the self-employed, by race and Hispanic origin, 1989

Race/ Ethnic Group	Average Annual Earnings ($)	As a Percent of Non-Hispanic White Earnings
Non-Hispanic White	$45,698	100.0
Black	27,082	59.3
Hispanic	29,960	65.6
Asian	46,438	101.6
Native American	26,954	59.0
Other	35,623	78.0

Source: Author's calculations from Bureau of the Census (1993).

non-Hispanic whites. For Hispanics the figure is 65.6 percent. For Native Americans, the figure is 59.0 percent. Enormous earnings disparities are apparent for all groups except Asians.

Although available data sources are more limited, there is also evidence of racial disparities between minority-owned and non-minority owned businesses, as opposed to individual business owners. Data from the 1987 and 1992 editions of *The Survey of Minority-Owned Business Enterprises* (Bureau of the Census 1991a; 1991b; 1991c; 1991d; 1996a; 1996b; 1996c; 1996d), presented below in Table 1.2 and Table 1.3, show large differentials between minority businesses and their non-minority counterparts.[21]

Table 1.2 shows the percentage of U.S. firms owned by non-minorities and minorities in 1987 and 1992. It also shows the percentage of annual aggregate sales and receipts earned by minority-owned and non-minority-owned firms in each year. Clearly, the market share of minority-owned businesses is much lower than would be expected based on their percentage availability in the market place. In 1987, minorities owned less than 9 percent of all firms and earned less than 4 percent of sales and receipts. By 1992, the availability of minority firms had grown to 11.4 percent of all U.S. firms. However, these firms still earned only 6.1 percent of all sales and receipts. One way to quantify the extent of these racial and ethnic disadvantages in business enterprise is to construct a disparity index. This is done by dividing market share (column B) by market availability (column A) and multiplying the result by one hundred. The resulting index appears in column C. An index value of one hundred would indicate perfect racial parity, while a value of zero indicates complete disparity. The smaller the resulting statistic, the larger the disparity.

The large disparities in Table 1.2 exemplify the marginal status of most large minority groups in American business enterprise activity. Market share levels for blacks and Hispanics never exceed even half of their corresponding availability levels. Asians face disparities as well, although not of the magnitude of those facing black and Hispanic business owners. Native Americans also face disparities in both years, although the magnitude of the disparity is quite different in both years.[22]

Another way to consider these disparities is in terms of average annual receipts per firm, as shown in Table 1.3.[23] This table shows that non-minority firms, on average, are substantially larger than minority-owned firms in terms of annual sales and receipts. In 1992, the average non-

Table 1.2. Minority firm population shares and market shares, 1987 and 1992

All Industries by Race/Ethnic Group	Minority Firms as a Percent of All U.S. Firms	Minority Sales and Receipts as a Percentage of All Sales and Receipts	Disparity Index — Column (B) as a Percentage of Column (A)
	(A)	(B)	(C)
1992			
Non-minority	88.61	93.92	106.0
Minority:	11.39	6.08	53.3
Black	3.60	0.97	26.9
Hispanic	4.47	2.19	49.0
Asian	3.27	2.83	86.3
Native	0.24	0.17	72.7
1987			
Non-minority	91.14	96.10	105.4
Minority:	8.86	3.90	44.0
Black	3.10	0.99	32.0
Hispanic	3.08	1.24	40.2
Asian	2.59	1.66	64.0
Native	0.16	0.05	29.3

Source: Author's calculations from Bureau of the Census (1991a; 1991b; 1991c; 1991d; 1996a; 1996b; 1996c; 1996d).

minority-owned firm within the survey universe grossed almost $193,000 in sales. The typical black-owned firm, on the other hand, grossed less than $52,000. Other minority groups also grossed far less, on average, than their non-minority counterparts in both 1987 and 1992.

Table 1.3. Average annual minority firm sales and receipts: absolute and relative to non-minority sales and receipts

Race/ Ethnic Group	Sales and Receipts	Disparity Index — Minority Sales as a Percentage of Non-minority Sales
1992		
Non-minority	$192,672	100.0
Minority	102,775	53.3
Black	51,855	26.9
Hispanic	94,368	49.0
Asian	166,205	86.3
Native	140,084	72.7
1987		
Non-minority	$145,654	100.0
Minority	64,132	44.0
Black	46,592	32.0
Hispanic	58,554	40.2
Asian	93,221	64.0
Native	42,623	29.3

Source: Author's calculations from Bureau of the Census (1991a; 1991b; 1991c; 1991d; 1996a; 1996b; 1996c; 1996d).

Do Business Enterprise Disparities Result from Discrimination?

Although economists agree and my own research confirms that racial and ethnic disparities in business enterprise and self-employment exist and that they are large, little agreement exists about whether such disparities are the result, in whole or in part, of discrimination. While many academic studies of the traits of minority business enterprises and minority business owners have been conducted,[24] only a handful have examined empirically whether discrimination accounts for a significant portion of the racial and ethnic disparities observed in business formation rates and business earnings. Borjas and Bronars (1989), Bates (1988), and Moore (1983) all report evidence of consumer discrimination against self-employed minorities. Meyer (1990), Fairlie and Meyer (1994; 1996), and Fujii and Hawley (1991), on the other hand, reach opposite conclusions. Together with a handful of the best disparity studies, these articles comprise the entire scholarly economics literature on this topic. None of the academic studies, however, has provided the geographic or the industrial detail that is implied under the new strict scrutiny standard.

Understanding the causes of racial and ethnic disparities in business enterprise is important not only for public policy purposes but is of economic interest in its own right since the existing research is not in agreement. If such differentials emerge due to unequal business opportunities caused by discrimination then the entire country pays a price resulting from decreased competition, underdeveloped human resources, and reduced social cohesion. Marshall (1991b, 10), for example, has observed that,

> The economic, political, and social health of any society depends heavily on access to economic and political power by all major racial, gender, and ethnic groups. . . .
> Business is a source of considerable economic and political power. To deny minorities and women access to this power on the basis of race or gender denies them full participation in the American system. Put another way, as long as minorities and women are denied access to business opportunities, the distribution of wealth, income, and power will continue to be unfair and even to polarize, with grave consequences for the economy, polity, and society.

Similarly, Fairlie and Meyer (1994, 1–2), note that

> Understanding the ethnic/racial character of self-employment is important for at least three reasons. First, conflicts between ethnic and racial groups in the U.S. have often been partly caused by business ownership patterns. . . . Second, self-employment has historically been a route of economic advancement for some ethnic groups. . . . Third, small business owners have an important effect on political decisions in the U.S. The under-representation of many ethnic/racial groups in

business means that these groups may possess less political power than is suggested by their proportion of the population.

Aronson (1991, 76–77) expressed similar concerns, noting, "[h]istorically, self-employment and small business ownership have been an important path by which ethnic, racial, and religious minorities in the United States have overcome social and cultural disabilities and entered the so-called mainstream."

It is to the further examination of the role of discrimination in racial and ethnic business disparities that the present study is directed. The purpose is to provide an objective examination of selected evidence on minority business enterprise in order to evaluate the economic content of the Supreme Court's new strict scrutiny standard. This will be accomplished by adapting the empirical techniques used by economists to investigate employment discrimination to the case of self-employment— or business—discrimination.

The remainder of the book is organized as follows. The first task will be to construct and evaluate for significance estimates of racial disparities in self-employment rates and earnings using 1990 census sample microdata according to geography, industry, and occupation. Next, three major questions are posed. The answers to these questions should be valuable both to public policy makers and to those jurists who are currently seeking to interpret the strict scrutiny standard in a manner that is both legally and economically sound. First, how much of the statistical disparity between minority and non-minority business owners can be accounted for by factors other than discrimination? Second, how sensitive are measures of minority business discrimination to differences in geography or industry? Finally, given the findings from the first two questions, does credible evidence of minority business discrimination exist at the level of racial, industrial, and geographic detail that the Supreme Court appears to require under *Croson's* strict scrutiny standard? Credible evidence is taken to mean evidence that would satisfy most economists.

Chapter two describes the data to be used in this study and produces a variety of estimates of gross racial and ethnic disparities in business enterprise and self-employment. A major focus of the chapter is an examination of whether racial self-employment disparities persist when the data are disaggregated by geography, industry, and occupation. Another major focus is on constructing geographically and industrially disaggregated estimates of minority business formation rates and the earnings of minority business owners as suggested by the *Croson* decision. To my knowledge, comparable estimates do not exist elsewhere in the literature.

Chapter three is concerned with adjusting the disparities documented in chapter two in order to estimate how much, if any, of each estimated differential remains unexplained after controlling for a variety of individual qualifications and characteristics, using procedures developed by Oaxaca and Ransom (1994) and Neumark (1988). This is taken as the measure of business discrimination. My maintained hypothesis is that discrimination persists even after these other factors have been accounted for.

Chapter three concludes with a summary of findings and an assessment of whether or not the differences in minority business discrimination across particular geographic, industrial, and occupational lines outweigh the similarities; and of whether the lower courts are applying the strict scrutiny standard in a manner that is consistent with the best available economic data.

NOTES

[1] The neoclassical theory of discrimination associated with Becker, Kenneth Arrow (1972a; 1972b) and others is thoroughly reviewed in Glen Cain (1986).

[2] And, by extension, through the institutions of other markets as well.

[3] See Ashenfelter and Oaxaca (1987) and Bloom and Killingsworth (1982) for good discussions of the use of econometric analysis in employment and wage discrimination litigation.

[4] Although, considering the foregoing discussion, such evidence certainly is relevant to furthering an understanding of how discrimination arises or how it can be changed.

[5] Blinder (1973) is an exception.

[6] The evidence continues to this day. See Wainwright (1991), Brimmer (1995), Enchautegui, *et al.* (1996) and Brimmer (1997).

[7] Important Supreme Court cases include *DeFunis v. Odegaard* (416 U.S. 312) in 1974 (higher education), *University of California Regents v. Bakke* in 1978 (higher education), *United Steelworkers of America v. Weber* (443 U.S. 193) in 1979 (employment, apprenticeship), *Wygant v. Jackson Board of Education* in 1985 (employment), and *Fullilove v. Klutznick* in 1980 (federal contracting and procurement).

[8] The Supreme Court and lower courts continue to extend the strict scrutiny standard to affirmative action for minorities in areas other than public contracting. For example, the 1993 decision in *Shaw v. Reno* (509 U.S. 630, 113 S.Ct. 2816) and the 1995 decision in *Miller v. Johnson* (115 S.Ct. 2475) invalidated U.S. congressional districts in North Carolina and Georgia, respectively, on the basis of strict scrutiny. In 1994, the Fourth Circuit Court of Appeals invalidated race-based educational scholarships on the basis of strict scrutiny in *Podberesky v. Kirwan* (38 F.3d 147). In 1995, the Fifth Circuit Court of Appeals appealed to strict scrutiny as it invalidated race-based university admissions policies in *Hopwood v. Texas* (78 F.3d 932).

[9] The constitutionality of a government's use of racial criteria, even when its motives are allegedly benign, is a controversial issue with a long history in constitutional law. The decisions in and subsequent to *Croson* are only the most recent events in this evolving area of constitutional interpretation. An in-depth examination of this area is beyond the scope of the present study. Ducat and Chase (1983, 679-901) together with Ducat (1978, 193-256) provide a good overview. More detail on the strict scrutiny standard and its two prongs in the context of MBE programs can be found in Abrams and Hayes (1990, 74-75), Bendick (1990, 94–100), Days (1990, 4–8), Goldstein (1990, 38–42), Marshall (1991b, 12–26), and Payton (1990, 21–29).

[10] According to the Census Bureau, blacks owned 7.5 percent of the construction businesses in the Richmond metropolitan area in 1987 and 7.2 percent in 1992 (Bureau of the Census 1991f; 1996f).

[11] In 1995, for example, bills were introduced in the 104th Congress that would eliminate all federal affirmative action in education, government contracting, and even employment (U.S. Congress, House 1995; U.S. Congress, Senate 1995). In January 1996, the Governor of Louisiana issued an executive order halting all state-sponsored affirmative action in Louisiana (Foster 1996). Following the lead of Governor Pete Wilson's 1995 Executive Order ending affirmative action in admissions at state universities, voters in the State of California approved by a substantial margin a referendum to abolish all state-sponsored affirmative action for minorities or women in employment, public contracting, and higher education (Wilson 1995; California Legislature 1996).

[12] The sources cited document approximately sixty studies. The author is personally aware of at least 15 additional studies that have been commissioned as of this writing.

[13] Alternatively, other approaches to the problem—such as outlawing private sector business discrimination outright (Marshall 1991b, 27), or establishing

pre-contract compliance review rating systems (Marshall 1991b, 28–31; Suggs 1990)—might be adopted in lieu of previous programs.

[14] Some disparity studies have attempted to circumvent this limitation by complementing statistical findings of gross disparities with supporting evidence from historical analyses and contemporary case studies (*e.g.* Brimmer and Marshall 1990).

[15] Unfortunately, in a few cases, data limitations have not been the only problem facing particular localities. In the Lunn and Perry study, for example, their conclusion that no discrimination was evident in the Louisiana highway construction industry is suspect since, among other things, their empirical results were based entirely on a mail survey of unknown sample properties with a 74 percent non-response rate (1993, 469). In another case, the Los Angeles County Metropolitan Transit Authority paid almost one million dollars for a disparity study that, under scrutiny by an outside panel of economists, turned out to be essentially worthless for purposes of meeting the strict scrutiny standard.

[16] There is a substantial body of economic and sociological literature from the late 1940s to the mid-1970s that describes the marginal nature of black business enterprise. These include Myrdal ([1944] 1962), Cayton and Drake (1946), Pierce (1947), Frazier (1957), Foley (1966), Farmer (1968), Brimmer (1966), and Coles (1969).

[17] Borjas' sample included employed males, age 18-64.

[18] Moore's sample included employed males, age 20-65, in the nonagricultural sector, who worked 35 or more hours per week and 31 or more weeks per year.

[19] The Borjas and Bronars sample included employed males, age 25-64, residing in the 75 largest Standard Metropolitan Statistical Areas.

[20] This sample is described in detail in chapter two and used extensively throughout the remainder of the present study. It includes self-employed males, age 25–64, employed in nonagricultural industries.

[21] The universe of businesses for the *Survey of Minority-Owned Business Enterprises* includes all sole proprietorships, partnerships and Subchapter S corporations. Other types of corporations are not included. See Wainwright (1991) for details.

[22] Although part of this change may be an artifact of the very small absolute magnitudes involved (*e.g.* Native American availability in 1987 is only 0.16 percent), part of it appears to be real. Inspection of unpublished tabulations from the 1992 SMOBE reveals extremely strong growth among Native American-owned firms in industry sectors such as mining and construction (Bureau of the Census 1996e).

[23] The resulting disparity ratios are, of course, equivalent to those appearing in Table 1.2.

[24] Bates (1993) provides an annotated bibliography covering the academic economics literature. Hill (1985) has authored a more extensive but largely unannotated bibliography covering, in addition to economics, the popular press, government documents, dissertations and theses, and scholarly journals in business, finance, sociology, and psychology.

CHAPTER 2

Documenting Business Disparities

This main purpose of this chapter is to estimate racial disparities in self-employment rates and earnings at a level of specificity that is more pertinent to the strict scrutiny standard than that found in existing academic research. This is a more interesting and relevant task than in the past due to the advent of *Croson*, and few available data sources are up to the task. The estimates in this chapter provide the unadjusted, or gross, racial and ethnic disparities with which the adjusted, or net, disparities will be compared in the next chapter to determine the relative importance of "qualifications" versus "discrimination" in accounting for racial differences in business enterprise activity.

Before turning to the estimates, I discuss three items in more detail: the importance of geographic and industrial detail in the current legal controversies involving affirmative action in government contracting, the strengths and weaknesses of the few data sources available for studying discrimination against minority-owned businesses, and the particular characteristics of the data source I chose to utilize for the present investigation.

INTRODUCTION: *CROSON* AND THE IMPORTANCE OF GEOGRAPHIC AND INDUSTRIAL DETAIL

Affirmative action for minority businesses proliferated rapidly in states and metropolitan areas across the country during the 1970s and 1980s. As mentioned in chapter one, by 1989 there were over 200 state and local government initiatives in place. This expansion was due in part to the U.S. Supreme Court's 1980 affirmation of the constitutionality of a congressionally mandated minority contracting set-aside in *Fullilove v. Klutznick.*

Fullilove involved a challenge to the Public Works Employment Act of 1977 (PWEA) (Pub. L. 95–28, 91 Stat. 116), which was the authorizing legislation for billions of dollars in federal-aid highway funds that Congress would release over the following five years. Before PWEA was passed, Congress held numerous hearings and received extensive testimony regarding discrimination against minority businesses in the construction industry. Partly as a result of these findings, Congress included provisions in the PWEA that required ten percent of highway transportation funds received under the act be spent with minority-owned businesses.

The MBE provisions of the PWEA were soon challenged in federal court as unconstitutional, and the case made it all the way to the Supreme Court. The Court, in an opinion authored by Chief Justice Warren E. Burger, upheld the constitutionality of the MBE provisions of the PWEA, and relied strongly on the congressional findings of nationwide discrimination in the construction industry in doing so. According to Stephanopoulos and Edley (1995, 45):

> In *Fullilove*, Chief Justice Burger reviewed the legislative history of the Public Works Employment Act of 1977 and its documentation of the extensive history of discrimination against minorities in contracting and especially federal procurement. The Chief Justice quoted from the 1977 Report of the House Committee on Small Business, which explored discrimination in contracting in the construction industry and found: "The very basic problem disclosed by the testimony is that, over the years, there has developed a business system which has traditionally excluded measurable minority participation." The report concluded that "minorities, until recently, have not participated to any measurable extent, in our total business system generally, or in the construction industry, in particular."

Many state and local governments, such as the City of Richmond, interpreted *Fullilove* as allowing them authority similar to that of the Congress to use their spending powers to combat racial discrimination against minority businesses within their jurisdictions, and to base their MBE affirmative action initiatives on the fact-finding studies previously undertaken by the Congress. But in 1989 the Supreme Court caught all of these governments by surprise when a 5–4 majority in *Croson* dramatically heightened the evidentiary and procedural standards required to support the constitutionality of a state or local—but not a federal—MBE program.

The *Croson* court ruled that aggregate *national* findings by Congress of minority business discrimination were not specific enough to support a MBE program in the City of Richmond. According to the Supreme Court, "[t]he probative value of these findings for demonstrating the existence of discrimination in Richmond is extremely limited" (*Croson* at 726). To support their conclusion, the Court noted that the federal MBE program, by including waivers and other provisions whereby MBE affirmative action requirements could be relaxed under certain conditions, "explicitly recognized that the scope of the problem would vary from market area to market area" (*ibid.*).[25] The Court appears to have concluded that anything less than an independent determination of discriminatory problems by every state or local agency wishing to operate a MBE program would no longer suffice to justify the constitutionality of such programs (*Croson* at 727):

> If all a state of local government need do is find a congressional report on the subject to enact a set-aside program, the constraints of the Equal Protection Clause will have been rendered a nullity. "It is essential that state and local agencies also establish the presence of discrimination in their own bailiwicks, based either upon their own fact-finding processes or upon determinations made by other competent institutions" [quoting Days (1990)].

Few if any state or local agencies had done any specific fact-finding of their own prior to the *Croson* ruling. As Bendick (1990, 94) observes:

> Prior to the *Croson* decision, many agencies and jurisdictions implementing race-conscious set-aside programs had done so without developing a detailed record to document discrimination in their locality . . . Instead, they had relied upon common knowledge and widely-recognized patterns, both local and national [reference omitted].

Furthermore, although its MBE program included blacks, Hispanics, Asians and Pacific Islanders, American Indians, Eskimos and Aleuts, the Court noted that the only evidence presented by the City of Richmond in defense of its program pertained to blacks. The *Croson* majority concluded that Richmond possessed no basis whatsoever for the inclusion of any other minority groups in its program.

It is evident that *Croson* represented a substantial departure from the precedents established in *Fullilove* for assessing the constitutionality of race-conscious affirmative action. The *Fullilove* majority appeared to recognize a systemic, or institutional, nature to discrimination in business enterprise while the *Croson* court appeared to see discrimination in much more particularized and discrete terms. Henceforth, state and local area governments are required to produce evidence of discrimination that relates to *specific minority groups* in *specific industries* in their *own local geographic area* rather than sharing in the findings of nationwide discrimination by Congress.

Tables 1.1, 1.2, and 1.3 document large racial and ethnic disparities in self-employment earnings and business enterprise market share, for the nation as a whole and across *all* industries. Since *Fullilove* has now been overturned, and *Croson* and *Adarand* are the law of the land, it is important to determine how these disparities change and if they persist when the data are disaggregated according to geography or industry. That is, do the disparities observed at the national level (such as those relied on by Congress in passing the MBE portions of the PWEA) result from relatively large differences concentrated in a relatively small number of locations, industries, or occupations, or are they observed across the entire spectrum? By how much do they vary from place to place and industry to industry and minority group to minority group? Finally, are these disparities, when observed, due to sampling variation and nothing more? And if not, are they large enough to be of practical policy concern?

A better understanding of how these measures behave at various levels of disaggregation and of their size and statistical significance is important if strict scrutiny is to be a practical standard for assessing constitutionality in the case of MBE affirmative action programs. The remainder of this chapter proceeds as follows. The next section introduces the primary dataset to be used in subsequent analyses, and discusses its strengths and weaknesses in comparison with other publicly available data. Using this dataset, in the final section I extend the estimates of disparities in self-employment rates and earnings presented in chapter one by geography and industry. I also conduct formal statistical tests to evaluate both the statistical significance and constitutional significance of the resulting estimates.

AVAILABLE DATA SOURCES FOR ANALYZING MINORITY BUSINESS ENTERPRISE

The publicly available data for analyzing minority business enterprise activity are quite limited—even when one does not consider the need for the large amount of geographic and industrial detail that is required under *Croson*. Historically, the most often used source has been the Census Bureau's *Survey of Minority Owned Business Enterprises*, or SMOBE (Bates 1993, 111). This is not surprising given that the SMOBE is the only regularly produced statistical series dedicated to collecting information on MBEs. Certain limitations of SMOBE, however, reduce its usefulness as a primary data source for analyzing the role of discrimination in explaining racial disparities in business enterprise in the context of *Croson*.

Several other data sources are also potentially relevant to an analysis of MBE issues. These include public sector contracting and procurement records, the *Characteristics of Business Owners* survey (Bureau of the Census 1991e), and the *Current Population Survey (e.g.* Census 1991g).[26] For purposes of strict scrutiny, however, these sources also have important limitations.

For reasons discussed below, the analyses presented here will be performed using data from the *1990 Census of Population and Housing 5% Public Use Microdata Samples*, or PUMS (Bureau of the Census 1993). Although the PUMS also has limitations when it comes to analyzing minority-owned businesses, it is nevertheless a rich and detailed data set with many important offsetting advantages. Because it is microdata, and because it includes hundreds or variables measuring social, economic, and demographic characteristics, it is suitable for the types of discrimination decomposition analyses described at the end of chapter one. Because it is so large, it provides more geographic, industrial, and occupational detail than any other available source of data. All this makes the PUMS relatively well suited for answering strict scrutiny inquiries arising out of the *Croson* decision.

I briefly review the various sources of data below before proceeding to a description of the particular PUMS sub-sample that will be used to conduct the analyses in the remainder of this study.

The Survey of Minority-Owned
Business Enterprises

The Census Bureau has published the SMOBE every five years since 1972 as part of its *Economic Censuses* program. The 1992 SMOBE, published in 1996, is the most recent available.[27] The SMOBE contains aggregate estimates of the number of minority-owned firms and their annual sales and receipts. The SMOBE distinguishes employer firms from nonemployer firms, and for the former also includes estimates of aggregate annual employment and payroll. Additionally, the SMOBE provides some limited information regarding the distribution of firms according to employment levels and receipts size.

Unlike most other business statistics, including the other components of the *Economic Censuses*, the unit of analysis in the SMOBE is the firm, rather than the establishment. The SMOBE estimates are created by matching data collected from income tax returns by the Internal Revenue Service with Social Security Administration data on race and ethnicity, and supplementing this information using statistical sampling methods. The unique field for conducting this matching is a person's Social Security Number (SSN), as reported on their tax return. Since corporations other than subchapter S corporations are not individually owned, no SSN appears on the tax return. Consequently, identifying the racial and ethnic characteristics of the corporate owners is not possible. For this reason, corporations other than Subchapter S are excluded from the SMOBE universe.

The SMOBE covers three groups of minorities—blacks, Hispanics, and a catch-all group including Asians, Pacific Islanders, and Native Americans (i.e., American Indians, Eskimos, and Aleuts). Since the 1987 survey, comparative information has also been provided for non-minority-owned firms.

The SMOBE obviously provides a wealth of information on the character of minority business enterprise. For a number of reasons, however, its usefulness from the standpoint of *Croson* and the strict scrutiny standard of the Supreme Court would be enhanced if certain weaknesses in the SMOBE were addressed. First, as mentioned above, due to the nature of the survey design, certain larger corporations are excluded from the survey universe. Second, although the SMOBE can be used to calculate certain unadjusted, or gross, disparities between minority and non-minority businesses, it does not include enough information to adjust these disparities for differences in productivity or other qualifications between firms. Third, Asians and Native Americans are grouped together in one category in the SMOBE. Also, because the underlying sample sizes are relatively small, the geographic and industrial detail available in SMOBE is more limited than in the PUMS. The geographic and industrial detail available in the SMOBE is summarized below in Table 2.1.

Consequently, while the SMOBE is very useful for establishing the initial magnitude of certain disparities, it is less suitable for a *Croson*-type analysis of discrimination as a factor contributing to racial disparities in business enterprise. It would be useful if future versions of SMOBE collected more information, used larger sample sizes, were conducted more frequently, and were processed more quickly.[28]

Table 2.1. Available geographic and industry detail in the *Survey of Minority-Owned Business Enterprises*

Geographic Detail	Industry Detail
Nation as a whole	All industries
Nation as a whole	Industry divisions (1-digit SIC)
Nation as a whole	Industry divisions (1-digit SIC)
Nation as a whole	Industry major groups (2-digit SIC)
States	All industries
States	Industry divisions
Metropolitan Areas	All industry
Metropolitan Areas	Industry divisions
Counties	All industry
Places	All industry

Note: "SIC" stands for Standard Industrial Classification.

Government Contracting and Procurement Data

Another important type of data for purposes of evaluating the constitutionality of MBE programs would be the contracting and procurement data of the government entities themselves, since this would track the activity among those businesses that are actually providing materials or services to the public sector in a given time period. Of course, this type of data is maintained separately by thousands of different public entities across the country. This type of data is also not generally made available to the public. Even if it were, each government compiles, tabulates, and classifies such data differently and over different time periods.

Most of the disparity studies mentioned in chapter one relied in part of data of this kind. The disparity study research team is typically given access to contracting and procurement data for purposes of conducting the study. A large amount of additional processing must be performed on such data until it is suitable for analysis. For example, before *Croson*, many government agencies with MBE programs did not keep records on the race or ethnicity of their contractors and vendors. Researchers from a disparity study team typically have to identify these factors retrospectively using secondary data and additional primary data.

Most of these disparity studies contain a wealth of statistical information based on the procurement records of individual government entities. Because they were compiled for different government entities at different times by different researchers, however, there are usually serious inconsistencies among these studies in the types of data used and the methods of analysis employed. Consistent sources of data on state and local government expenditures, such as the *Census of Governments* and the *Government Finances* series are available, but none of these contains any information regarding the race and ethnicity of government contractors and vendors.

Despite these empirical challenges, most disparity studies have documented large racial and ethnic disadvantages in government contracting and procurement. A recent report by the Urban Institute summarized and evaluated almost 60 of these studies. The U.S. Department of Justice commissioned that report, with assistance from the Rockefeller Foundation, as part of the federal government's effort to respond to the *Adarand* decision. Principal among the report's findings was the following (Enchautegui, et al. 1996, v-vi):

We find substantial disparity in government contracting. That is, minority-owned businesses receive far fewer government contract dollars than would be expected based on their availability. Minority-owned businesses as a group receive only 57 cents of each dollar that they would be expected to receive . . . Further, there is substantial disparity in government contracting for each minority population group [black, Hispanic, Asian and Native American] . . . Disparity exists in every industry group studied as well.

The Characteristics of Business Owners Survey

The *Characteristics of Business Owners* (CBO) survey was conducted concurrently with the SMOBE in 1982, 1987, and 1992. The CBO is derived primarily from a mail survey sent by the Census Bureau to a subsample of firms covered by the SMOBE. The object of the CBO is to link the information on the firm from SMOBE with information on the firm's owner provided by the mail survey. According to Bates (1993, 117–18),

> The CBO is unlike any other large-scale small business survey that has been undertaken to date. Other sources, such as the [PUMS], which uses samples from the decennial population census, describe self-employed people as individuals; periodic business census data describe businesses. The CBO survey is the first very large survey data base that describes self-employed people as individuals as well as the traits of the firms these people own . . . .

Table 2.2 summarizes the large amount of personal information, labor market information, and financial information the CBO survey solicited from business owners in five categories—black, Hispanic, other minority, female, and non-minority male. The CBO data are presented for each of the five race or sex groups according to (a) industry division, (b) receipts size, (c) employment size, and (d) legal form of organization.

Unfortunately for those who might want to utilize this survey for strict scrutiny purposes, the CBO's findings are published in the aggregate only and no geographic detail is available below the national level. There is, however, a microdata counterpart to the published CBO. This microdata represents an potentially important source of information regarding MBEs and their non-minority counterparts. Unfortunately, the CBO microdata are not publicly available. As Bates (1993, 117–119) notes:

Table 2.2. Information collected in *Characteristics of Business Owners Survey*

Personal information:	Age, marital status, birthplace, education, disability, military status, personal income
Labor market information:	Work experience, business experience, labor supply, percent of employees that are female, percent of employees that are minority, percent of customers that are minority
Financial information:	Household income, contribution of business to household income, years in business, method by which business was acquired, required starting capital, amount and source of debt financing, assets, liabilities, net income or loss

> Gaining access to the [CBO] data, however, is not easy. It requires gaining the appropriate government security clearances, paying $200 per day to use Census Bureau facilities, and working in the Suitland, Maryland, headquarters building of the Census Bureau. In light of the tremendous potential value of the CBO data . . . the inaccessibility is tragic.

The Current Population Survey

The *Current Population Survey* (CPS) has many features in common with the PUMS. Like the PUMS, it is publicly available at a nominal charge. It covers approximately the same universe as the PUMS and includes most of the same variables—including the class of worker variable necessary to identify the self-employed. The biggest advantage of the CPS is that it is available as an annual time series, covering 1970–95, as opposed to once every ten years as with the PUMS.[29] The time series nature of the data is especially attractive because the self-employed share of the labor force has increased substantially in recent years (Aronson 1991, 1–19). Also, there is some limited evidence from the SMOBE indicating—with the notable exception of blacks—that minority-owned businesses have been growing faster in recent years than their non-minority counterparts.[30]

On the other hand, the CPS sample size is much smaller than the PUMS, and this limits both the geographic and industrial detail available and the precision of any estimates. The CPS is constructed from a sample of approximately 70,000 housing units. The resulting database contains information on approximately 160,000 individuals (Bureau of the Census 1991g). However, considering that about 34,000 of these individuals are under age 16, and that the overall self-employment rate is only about 12 percent, the number of actual observations available for analysis is quite limited when considering the racial, ethnic, geographic, and industrial detail that may be required in any particular instance.[31] In contrast, the PUMS, to which I now turn, is constructed from a sample of over 5.5 million housing units containing more than 12.5 million persons.

Public Use Microdata Samples from the Decennial Census

The main dataset used for this project was drawn from the 1990 5 percent PUMS. The PUMS contains observations representing 5 percent of all U.S. housing units, and the persons in them. The PUMS, released in late 1993, provides the full range of population and housing information collected in the 1990 census (Bureau of the Census 1992a; 1993).[32]

The PUMS includes numerous variables measuring influences that have been identified as important by others who have researched self-employment phenomena. These variables are summarized in Table 2.3. Aronson (1991) provides a review of what is presently known about these various influences, several of which will be included in the analyses presented in chapter three, below.

Business ownership is identified in the PUMS through the "class of worker" variable, which distinguishes the unincorporated and incorporated self-employed from other types of employed persons. The presence

Table 2.3. Information collected in *Public Use Microdata Samples*

Personal information:	Age, education, sex, race, Hispanic origin, marital status, children, military service, disability, immigrant status, English language proficiency
Labor market information:	Employment status, class of worker, hours and weeks usually worked, industry, occupation, geographic location
Financial information:	Household income, personal income, earnings, income from wage and salary work, income from self-employment, dividend and interest income, selected housing costs, property value

of the class of worker variable allows one to construct a rich and detailed cross-sectional sample of individual business owners and their earnings. Presently, the PUMS may be the only publicly available data source large enough and diverse enough to allow econometric methods to be applied to local-area and/or industry-specific investigations of minority business ownership with enough statistical precision to produce reliable results.

Racial and Ethnic Detail in the PUMS. In part because they have relied on SMOBE, and in part because it is a very traditional scheme, the vast majority of disparity studies disaggregate race and ethnicity into four mutually exclusive categories: (1) white; (2) black; (3) Hispanic; and (4) "other" (including Asians, Native Americans, and other minority groups).

For many purposes, this scheme is probably sufficient for non-Hispanic whites and blacks. Most demographic experts, however, believe that the "Hispanic" and "Asian American" and Native American" categories inappropriately combine numerous racial and ethnic subgroups that are themselves quite diverse. Regarding "Hispanics," according to Bean and Tienda (1987, 7):

> Although common ancestral ties to Spain and/or Latin America, as well as frequent usage of the Spanish language, might seem to imply an underlying cultural similarity among peoples of Hispanic origin, the diverse settlement and immigration experiences of Mexicans, Puerto Ricans, Cubans, and other Hispanic groups have created distinct subpopulations with discernible demographic and economic characteristics. Persisting socioeconomic differences among these groups not only challenge the idea that the term 'Hispanic' is appropriate as an ethnic label, they also suggest that a careful scrutiny of the historical commonalities and divergencies among these groups as they have settled in the United States is relevant to understanding their contemporary socio-demographic situations.

Similar conclusions were drawn by Herbert Barringer and his colleagues regarding Asian Americans and Pacific Islanders (Barringer, Gardner, and Levine 1993, 17):

> On every dimension we have studied, Asian Americans vary as much as or more than the total American population. This is true of their de-

mographic characteristics, geographical distribution, migration history, and socioeconomic characteristics. . . . [T]he characteristics of each of the major Asian ethnic groups are so different from each other, that it becomes impossible to make intelligent (or intelligible) generalizations about Asian Americans as a whole. . . . The same may be said about Pacific Islanders, and certainly we shall avoid the temptation to say anything about Asian *and* Pacific Islander Americans in the same breath [Barringer, Gardner, and Levine's italics].

Finally, for Native Americans, Snipp (1989, 39–40) has noted:

In many respects, the groups included in the American Indian population are extremely diverse. American Indians in the Pacific Northwest have little in common with Indians of the Southwest or Southeast. . . . The same . . . applies to American Indians and Alaska Natives. In fact, Alaska Natives have very little in common with the tribal cultures found in the lower 48 states. Evidence of the cultural diversity within the American Indian population is abundant . . . .

In contrast to the SMOBE, the 1990 PUMS distinguishes sixty-two different racial groups. The PUMS provides additional racial detail for the Asian and Pacific Islander groups and for the Native American groups. The PUMS also includes more than thirty distinct codes classifying persons of Hispanic origin.

Concerning these minority groups, the PUMS is capable of much more racial and ethnic disaggregation than is possible with the SMOBE or the other data sources discussed above. Using PUMS, "Hispanic" Americans can be disaggregated into more homogeneous sub-populations, as can Asian Americans, Pacific Islanders, and Native Americans.[33]

For present purposes, since the exposition is already complicated by the need to consider a great deal of geographic, industrial, and occupational detail, and since this particular issue is not the focus of the present investigation, I will maintain these admittedly artificial racial and ethnic categories for Hispanics, Native Americans, and Asians, and reserve a more detailed investigation for the future. A virtue of the present scheme is its separate treatment of Asians and Native Americans (in contrast to the SMOBE), and its consistency with the types of racial and ethnic groupings commonly found in affirmative action legislation as well as in judicial interpretation of such legislation.

Geographic Detail in the PUMS. Geographically, the PUMS includes all fifty states and the District of Columbia. The basic geographic unit in the PUMS is the Public Use Microdata Area (PUMA). To make microdata publicly available without violating the strict confidentiality laws that cover the release of individual decennial census records, no geographic detail is provided below the PUMA level. Each PUMA was constructed to contain at least 100,000 persons. Each PUMA is typically a county or group of counties, depending on population density. In the most densely populated areas, a PUMA may represent only a portion of a county (Bureau of the Census 1992a). PUMAs can be combined to produce estimates for all states and the District of Columbia, most Consolidated Metropolitan Statistical Areas (CMSA), Primary Metropolitan Statistical Areas (PMSA), Metropolitan Statistical Areas (MSA), and for many cities and counties as well.

The PUMA geography in the 1 percent PUMS is arranged to allow slightly better identification of complete MSAs and complete central cities than the 5 percent PUMS. This is because in the 5 percent sample certain PUMAs contain a mix of MSA and non-MSA components. The Boston CMSA, for example, is composed of 37 separate PUMAs. Of these 37 PUMAs, 32 are contained entirely within the CMSA. The five remaining PUMAs included observations from metropolitan as well as nearby non-metropolitan areas. All told, these non-metropolitan observations represent an additional 160,000 persons out of a CMSA population of over 4.6 million—about 3.5 percent of the total.

The ability of the 1 percent PUMS to discriminate more finely at the CMSA, PMSA, MSA, and central city levels, however, comes at the cost of a much smaller sample size. Furthermore, the 1 percent PUMS identifies whole states with slightly less precision than does the 5 percent PUMS. For these reasons, I find the 5 percent sample more suitable than the 1 percent sample for present purposes.

Industry Detail in the PUMS. The 1990 PUMS classifies employed persons into 235 distinct industry categories which, in turn, are aggregated into thirteen summary categories (Bureau of the Census 1992a). The census classification is based on the 1987 Standard Industrial Classification (SIC) scheme. In most cases, the 235 industry categories correspond to SIC *major groups*, also known as two-digit SIC codes. The thirteen summary categories correspond roughly to SIC *industry divisions*, also known as one-digit SIC codes. To keep the exposition tractable, the detail presented in this chapter will be limited to the industry division level. These thirteen industry divisions are listed below in Table 2.4.[34]

Table 2.4. Primary industry groups used in the 1990 PUMS

Primary Industry Groups	
1. Agriculture, forestry, and fisheries	7. Retail trade
	8. Finance, insurance, and real estate
2. Mining	9. Business and repair services
3. Construction	10. Personal services
4. Manufacturing	11. Entertainment and recreation services
5. Transportation, communications, and public utilities	
	12. Professional and related services
6. Wholesale trade	13. Public administration

Occupational Detail in the PUMS. The occupational classification developed for the 1990 PUMS contains 501 separate categories for employed persons. These categories are subdivided into six summary groups and thirteen major groups as outlined in Table 2.5. As with industry detail, to keep the results manageable the findings presented in this chapter will be limited to the thirteen major groups described in the classification scheme.[35]

THE DATASET PREPARED FOR THIS STUDY

Sample Composition

Table 2.6 (line 1) shows that the 1990 PUMS contains observations on 12,501,046 persons in the general population. To focus on racial and ethnic dimensions of self-employed business owners, I have restricted the sample along several important dimensions.

First, the sample includes only men. The exclusion of women does not indicate that business disparities are insignificant or unimportant among women. To the contrary, there is substantial evidence of disparities in business enterprise between women and men—without regard to race or ethnicity (Aronson 1991, 60)—as well as among women businesses according to race and ethnicity (Fairlie and Meyer 1996, 761–763). Rather, the sample was restricted to men for several reasons. First, such a restriction avoids confounding race discrimination with gender discrimination. This is important for present purposes since the strict scrutiny

Table 2.5. Primary occupational groups used in the 1990 PUMS

I.	Managerial and Professional Specialty Occupations
	A. Executive, Administrative, and Managerial Occupations
	B. Professional Specialty Occupations
II.	Technical, Sales, and Administrative Support Occupations
	A. Technicians and Related Support Occupations
	B. Sales Occupations
	C. Administrative Support Occupations
III.	Service Occupations
	A. Private Household Occupations
	B. Protective Service Occupations
	C. Other Service Occupations
IV.	Farming, Forestry, and Fishing Occupations
V.	Precision Production, Craft, and Repair Occupations
	A. Construction Trades
	B. Other Precision Production, Craft, and Repair Occupations
VI.	Operators, Fabricators, and Laborers
	A. Machine Operators, Assemblers, and Inspectors
	B. Transportation and Material Moving Occupations

standard does not apply to gender-based affirmative action.[36] Also, since the focus of the present research is on employed persons (the self-employed on the one hand and wage and salary workers on the other), excluding women eliminates the complicating factor of having to model the well-known differences in labor supply and occupational-choice behavior between women and men (Pencavel 1986; Killingsworth and Heckman 1986).

After restricting the sample to men, the next step is to recognize that the labor supply behavior of the young and the retired is different from those of prime working age (Lazear 1986; Weiss 1986). Consequently, the sample is restricted to persons between the ages of 25–64. This is in keeping with most existing self-employment research, for example Fairlie and Meyer (1996), Bernhardt (1994), Fujii and Hawley (1991), Borjas and Bronars (1989), and Moore (1983). As shown in Table 2.6 (line 2), imposing these sex and age restrictions on the complete 1990 PUMS leaves 3,035,626 records in the sample, representing approximately 61 million prime working age males.

Several additional restrictions were imposed in creating the PUMS sample for this study. First, persons residing in PUMAs classified as entirely non-metropolitan were excluded, since of the hundreds of state and local MBE affirmative action programs that have been implemented during the last twenty years or so, few if any have been sponsored by non-metropolitan governmental jurisdictions. Restricting the data to metropolitan areas also allows, in the next chapter, for matching the PUMS data to proxy measures of local labor market conditions that are generally available only for metropolitan areas.

Second, the sample excludes persons who—voluntarily or involuntarily—did not work in 1989, which is the reference year for the income and earnings variables. It would be interesting to examine the patterns of unemployment behavior between the self-employed and wage and salary workers for differences. Although there is evidence that when modeling employment sector choice, as I do in the next chapter, it is important to include the non-market sector in the model (Heckman and Sedlacek 1990), this greatly complicates the entire analysis and I leave this complication for future research.

Third, since they have no counterparts in the self-employment sector, I excluded persons employed in the non-profit sector, the public sector (including the military), or as unpaid family workers. Fourth, since self-employment behavior in the agricultural sector is likely to be different from that in the nonagricultural sector, persons employed in agricultural industries were excluded from the dataset.[37] This is in keeping with most of the modern literature on self-employment.

Table 2.6. Scope of sub-sample restrictions imposed on the 1990 PUMS to create the data used in this study

Restriction	Number of Observations
1. Total general population	12,501,046
2. Males only, age 25–64	3,035,626
3. Residing in metropolitan areas	2,428,851
4. Worked in 1989	2,205,393
5. For pay, nonagricultural, for-profit, private sector	1,713,264
6. Full-time, year-round	1,441,129

Source: Author's calculations from Bureau of the Census (1993).

After imposing the above restrictions, the sample contains 1,713,264 observations, representing approximately 36.2 million men. This figure is within one percent of similarly restricted labor force estimates for 1990 from the CPS (Bureau of the Census 1991i, 27, 384, 392–93, 401).

Finally, it is likely that the part-time self-employed, most of whom are multiple jobholders, do not correspond very closely to the going concerns measured in other data sources such as SMOBE (Aronson 1991, 84–85). Thus, I have also identified those persons in the sample working full-time (35 hours per week or more) and year-round (40 weeks per year or more). The existing literature is not consistent in this regard. Bernhardt (1994) and Moore (1983) both exclude persons working part-time (although their definitions of "part-time" differ). Fujii and Hawley (1991), Borjas and Bronars (1989), Bates (1988), and Bearse (1984) do not exclude such persons. In this project, I will follow Fairlie and Meyer (1996), whose data set was constructed to allow for the inclusion or exclusion of part-time employment as necessary. In my data set, 1,441,129 observations—84.1 percent—represent men who worked full-time and year-round in 1989 (Table 2.6, line 6).

Sample Weights, Clustering, and Stratification

An additional aspect of the PUMS is that it includes sample probability weights. This is because the 1990 decennial census long form—which is the form used to collect the most economically interesting census information, such as income and earnings—is a stratified cluster sample of persons within housing units. Strata were sampled at different rates ranging from 1-in-2 to 1-in-8. The overall sample rate was approximately 1-in-6. The 1990 PUMS, in turn, is a random sample drawn from this long form universe and representing 5 percent of all U.S. housing units.

The 1990 PUMS includes a weight for each observation reflecting the full long form census sample weighting. Applying these weights allows data users to produce PUMS estimates that have conditional expectations (given the census sample) equal to the full census sample estimates (Thompson 1992; Kish 1965). This weighting scheme reduces the PUMS sample bias, leading to more efficient estimates. PUMS probability weights, clusters, and strata are applied throughout the remainder of this study.[38]

ESTIMATES OF NATION-WIDE AND ECONOMY-WIDE DISPARITIES IN RACIAL AND ETHNIC SELF-EMPLOYMENT RATES AND EARNINGS

In this section I use the dataset described above to estimate self-employment rates in 1990 by race and Hispanic origin. Estimates are presented first for the nation and the economy as a whole, and then at progressively finer levels of detail. At least three purposes are served by the production of estimates in this manner. First, the estimates can be evaluated to see if racial and ethnic disparities in self-employment persist as the data are disaggregated. Second, the standard errors of these estimates can be evaluated at various levels of disaggregation in order to gauge the magnitude of the loss in point estimate precision that occurs as successively finer levels of geographic and economic detail are considered. Third, the estimates have value in their own right. As several researchers have noted, there is little if any published data regarding racial and ethnic self-employment at this level of geographic or industry detail (Aronson 1991, 77–78; Borjas and Bronars 1989, 602).

I follow Aronson in defining self-employment as an alternative means of earning a living through the sale of one's labor. As he observes (1991, xi–xii):

> . . . most self-employed workers are not entrepreneurs in the classic sense, that is, individuals with a unique mission of breaking new ground in the production and/or distribution of goods and services. Rather, wisely or otherwise and for a variety of reasons, they have chosen to work for themselves. . . . [It is] the degree of autonomy and control these workers have over their labor which, in my view, theoretically distinguishes self-employment from wage and salary employment.

By "classic," Aronson is referring to the Schumpeterian notion of the entrepreneur, which views entrepreneurs as innovators and arbitrageurs (Schumpeter [1912] 1961). The "classic" entrepreneur of Knight ([1921] 1965), on the other hand, for whom profits are a return to a unique (*i.e.*, uninsurable) form of risk-bearing, is more consistent with Aronson's concept of autonomy and control over one's labor than is the Schumpeterian one.[39] The "earnings" of the self-employed thus include the wages of labor as well as the profits of enterprise.

Self-Employment Rates
by Race and Hispanic Origin

Self-employment has been measured in different ways in different data sources and by the various researchers using these sources. For example, several important sources of data on self-employment, such as the CPS, classify incorporated business owners as wage and salary workers rather than self-employed. Excluding incorporated firms will obviously lower any estimate of the number of self-employed persons or of self-employment rates. Furthermore, as discussed in more detail below, since incorporated firms are often larger and older than unincorporated firms, their exclusion from measured self-employment earnings would tend to make self-employment appear to be a less lucrative alternative to wage and salary work than is actually the case.

The measure of self-employment adopted here includes both the unincorporated *and* the incorporated self-employed. As discussed previously, it is restricted to the private and for-profit sectors of the economy and to the nonfarm and metropolitan sectors of the economy. Eliminated were the relatively young, the relatively old, women, and the unemployed. Also eliminated, implicitly, are persons employed in the informal sector. All but this last restriction were imposed to increase the likelihood that the self-employed persons contained in the resulting sample would be as representative as possible of the population of male business enterprise owners in the U.S.

Table 2.7 presents estimates from the PUMS of the total number of self-employed and wage and salary workers by race and Hispanic origin for the nation and the economy as a whole in 1990. Table 2.8 presents similar estimates for the full-time, year-round subset described earlier. Several aspects of these tables are worth noting.

One important aspect is the extremely large overall sample size. There are more than 1.7 million records in the overall dataset and more than 1.4 million in the full-time subset. There are almost 251,000 records on the self-employed in the overall dataset and more than 202,000 in the full-time subset. Sample sizes for most minority groups are also very large. In the overall dataset, there are almost 121,000 observations on non-Hispanic blacks and more than 140,000 observations on Hispanics. Considering just the self-employed among these two groups, there are over 8,000 observations on self-employed blacks and more than 13,000 observations on self-employed Hispanics. In the full-time subset, there are almost 5,500 observations on self-employed blacks out of a total of just over 91,000; and almost 10,000 observations on self-employed Hispanics out of a total of more than 109,000.

The sample sizes for Asians and Native Americans are smaller than for blacks and Hispanics, reflecting their smaller shares in the overall U.S. population. On the other hand, they are much larger than those found in other potential sources of minority business data such as the CPS or the SMOBE.

Table 2.7. Estimated self-employment and wage and salary employment, by race and Hispanic origin, 1990

Class of Worker and Race/Ethnic Group	Sample Size	%	Population Size	%
All Employed:	1,713,264		36,235,102	
Self-employed	250,985	14.7	5,153,722	14.2
Wage and salary	1,462,279	85.4	31,081,380	85.8
Self-employed:				
Non-Hispanic white	219,463	87.4	4,454,487	86.4
Non-Hispanic black	8,252	3.3	202,429	3.9
Hispanic, any race	13,347	5.3	287,086	5.6
Non-Hispanic Asian	8,815	3.5	187,628	3.6
Non-Hisp. Native Amer.	928	0.4	18,129	0.4
Non-Hispanic other race	180	0.1	3,963	0.1
Wage and Salary Workers:				
Non-Hispanic white	1,169,219	80.0	24,343,670	78.3
Non-Hispanic black	112,555	7.7	2,785,063	9.0
Hispanic, any race	126,731	8.7	2,786,852	9.0
Non-Hispanic Asian	45,129	3.1	987,135	3.2
Non-Hisp. Native Amer.	7,106	0.5	144,335	0.5
Non-Hispanic other race	1,539	0.1	34,335	0.1

Source: Author's calculations from Bureau of the Census (1993).

Notes: (1) Includes males, age 25–64, residing in metropolitan areas, employed for pay in 1989, working in the for-profit, private, nonagricultural sector; (2) Numbers may not add to total due to rounding.

In addition to sample size issues, Tables 2.7 and 2.8 also provide initial point estimates for self-employment rates—overall and by race and Hispanic origin. The percentage estimates vary slightly depending on whether they are based on the raw sample numbers or the full census population estimates. This is due to the use of the sample weights, discussed above, in calculating the population estimates. These weights reflect, among other things, a certain amount of sample stratification by age, race, Hispanic origin, and family status.

Table 2.7 documents a self-employment rate for employed prime working age males of 14.2 percent for 1990. For those employed full-time and year-round the corresponding estimate is 13.6 percent. The difference between these two rates reflects a substantially higher self-employment rate among the part-time employed—17.4 percent—than among the full-time employed. These national level estimates are very precise. For the overall dataset, a 99 percent confidence interval for the estimated self-employment rate runs approximately from 14.1 percent to 14.3 percent. For the full-time employed and self-employed the corresponding interval is 13.5 percent to 13.7 percent.

These estimated self-employment rates are substantially higher than those reported elsewhere for men. Using Social Security Administration data on covered employment, Aronson (1991, 5) estimated male self-employment in 1986 at 10.8 percent. A large part of the difference between my estimate and Aronson's is accounted for by the exclusion of 16–24 year olds from the sample. The self-employment rate for this age group is far below that for any other group. As Silvestri (1991, 29) has noted, "[t]he distribution of self-employed workers by age [in 1990] was very similar to that for total employment. The major difference was the percentage of workers age 16 to 24—only 4.5 percent for the self-employed versus 16.8 percent for total employment." Further, the Social Security Administration data used by Aronson do not include the incorporated self-employed. This directly biases estimated self-employment rates downward relative to those in my own sample.

Finally, the difference between Aronson's estimates and my own may also be partly due to secular growth in self-employment rates. Aronson has documented the resurgence in nonagricultural self-employment rates that began in the mid-1970s (1991, 2–5) after almost a century of decline. This growth trend has continued into the present. This can be seen from a comparison with estimated self-employment rates from Borjas and Bronars (1989, 594). Borjas and Bronars' sample was drawn from the 1980 PUMS and is very similar to my own in terms of the sex,

**Table 2.8. Estimated self-employment and wage and salary employ-
ment, by race and Hispanic origin, 1990 (full-time, year-round
workers only)**

Class of Worker and Race/Ethnic Group	Sample Size	%	Population Size	%
All Employed:	1,441,129		30,422,177	
Self-employed	202,225	14.0	4,142,795	13.6
Wage and salary	1,238,904	86.0	26,279,382	86.4
Self-employed:				
Non-Hispanic white	178,840	88.4	3,626,698	87.5
Non-Hispanic black	5,480	2.7	133,738	3.2
Hispanic, any race	9,777	4.8	211,065	5.1
Non-Hispanic Asian	7,348	3.6	155,768	3.8
Non-Hisp. Native Amer.	640	0.3	12,444	0.3
Non-Hispanic other race	140	0.1	3,082	0.1
Wage and Salary Workers:				
Non-Hispanic white	1,010,160	81.5	21,030,454	80.0
Non-Hispanic black	85,755	6.9	2,118,842	8.1
Hispanic, any race	99,493	8.0	2,189,893	8.3
Non-Hispanic Asian	37,088	3.0	807,312	3.1
Non-Hisp. Native Amer.	5,196	0.4	105,644	0.4
Non-Hispanic other race	1,212	0.1	27,237	0.1

Source: Author's calculations from Bureau of the Census (1993).

Notes: (1) Includes males, age 25–64, residing in metropolitan areas, employed
for pay in 1989, working in the for-profit, private, nonagricultural sector for 35
hours or more per week and for 40 or more weeks per year; (2) Numbers may
not add to total due to rounding.

age, industry, and other restrictions described previously. They estimate
the white male self-employment rate in 1980 to be 11.8 percent, versus
15.5 percent in my own sample.[40]

Tables 2.7 and 2.8 also provide estimates of the racial and ethnic
composition of the wage and salary worker pool versus that of the self-

employed.[41] For example, while blacks comprise 7.7 percent of employed wage and salary workers, they make up only 3.3 percent of the self-employed. When part-time employment is excluded, the percentages are 6.9 percent and 2.7 percent, respectively. A similar disparity is evident for Hispanics. Hispanics comprise 8.7 percent of the wage and salary work force but only 5.3 percent of the self-employed. When part-time employment is excluded, the percentages for Hispanics are 8.0 percent and 4.8 percent, respectively.

Although it is impossible to tell from Table 2.7 or Table 2.8, this trend is present for Native Americans and persons of "other race" as well. Due to the very small populations involved, however, these estimates should be treated with some caution. For example, Native Americans comprised 0.46 percent of all wage and salary workers in 1990, but only 0.35 percent of the self-employed. Persons of "other race" made up 0.11 percent of wage and salary workers but only 0.08 percent of the self-employed.

This pattern of lower minority representation among the pool of self-employed than among the pool of wage and salary workers is not evident for Asians. Indeed, Asians comprise a somewhat larger share of the pool of self-employed than of wage and salary workers. They constituted 3.1 percent of wage and salary workers and 3.5 percent of business owners in 1990. Among the full-time year-round subset, the figures are 3.0 and 3.6, respectively.

In Table 2.9, the numbers in Table 2.7 have been rearranged to provide the initial point estimates of self-employment rates by race and Hispanic origin. These are presented along with 95 percent confidence intervals for the estimated rates, sample sizes, and estimated population sizes.

Table 2.9 shows that the estimated self-employment rate for non-Hispanic whites in the sample, at 15.5 percent, is almost 2.3 times greater than the self-employment rate for blacks. Put differently, the black self-employment rate is only about 44 percent of the non-Hispanic white self-employment rate. The estimated self-employment rate for Hispanics is only about 60 percent of the non-Hispanic white rate. For Native Americans, the corresponding figure is about 72 percent. The Asian self-employment rate, on the other hand, is slightly higher than the non-Hispanic white rate. Each of these differences is statistically significantly different from zero, indicating that these differences are very unlikely to be due to chance. The probability of Type I error is less than 5-in-1000 (*i.e.* $p < 0.005$) for each estimated difference.[42, 43]

Table 2.9. Estimated self-employment rate, by race and Hispanic origin, 1990

Race/ Ethnic Group	Self- Employment Rate	Confidence Interval (Lower 95%)	Confidence Interval (Lower 95%)	Sample Size	Population Size
NH White	15.47	15.40	15.53	1,388,682	28,798,157
Black	6.78	6.62	6.93	120,807	2,987,492
Hispanic	9.34	9.17	9.51	140,078	3,073,938
Asian	15.97	15.63	16.31	53,944	1,174,763
Native	11.16	10.39	11.93	8,034	162,454
Other	10.35	8.76	11.94	1,719	38,298
Total	14.22	14.17	14.28	1,713,264	36,235,102

Source: Author's calculations from Bureau of the Census (1993).

Notes: (1) Includes males, age 25–64, residing in metropolitan areas, employed for pay in 1989, working in the for-profit, private, nonagricultural sector. Numbers may not add to total due to rounding; (2) "NH" stands for "Non-Hispanic"; (3) Hispanics can be of any race.

Except for Asians, each of these differences also exceeds the four-fifths threshold for substantiality adopted by the Equal Employment Opportunity Commission—and subsequently by several courts—for assessing the significance of racial differences in the wage and salary employment setting.[44] This so-called "80 percent rule" has been fairly widely endorsed as a more relevant way to gauge legally meaningful racial disparities than simply testing for statistical significance alone. According to Meier, Sacks, and Zabell (1986, 32):

> Properly understood, the 80% rule has the potential to rationalize much of the case law to date. . . . As a practical matter, even when statistically significant differences have been noted, the courts have been reluctant to find adverse impact when the differences lack what is variously described as "practical," "substantive," or "constitutional" significance. And conversely, substantial disparities have been found insufficient to establish a prima facie case when the sample sizes are so small as to make statistical significance unlikely. The 80% rule appears to be a reasonable articulation of a statistical criterion to determine whether statistically significant differences are substantial enough to warrant legal liability.

Table 2.10. **Estimated self-employment rate, by race and Hispanic origin, 1990 (full-time, year-round workers only)**

Race/ Ethnic Group	Self-Employment Rate	Confidence Interval (Lower 95%)	Confidence Interval (Lower 95%)	Sample Size	Population Size
NH White	14.71	14.64	14.78	1,189,000	24,657,152
Black	5.94	5.77	6.10	91,235	2,252,580
Hispanic	8.79	8.61	8.97	109,270	2,400,958
Asian	16.17	15.80	16.55	44,436	963,080
Native	10.54	9.67	11.41	5,836	118,088
Other	10.17	8.41	11.92	1,352	30,319
Total	13.62	13.56	13.68	1,441,129	30,422,177

Source: Author's calculations from Bureau of the Census (1993).

Notes: (1) Includes males, age 25–64, residing in metropolitan areas, employed for pay in 1989, working in the for-profit, private, nonagricultural sector for 35 hours or more per week and for 40 or more weeks per year. Numbers may not add to total due to rounding; (2) "NH" stands for "Non-Hispanic"; (3) Hispanics can be of any race.

The 80 percent rule states that for statistical disparities to be taken as legally dispositive in the discrimination context, they should be (a) statistically significant, generally at a two-sided, five percent (or corresponding one-sided, 2.5 percent) level; and (b) "substantively" significant. Substantive significance is taken to mean a minority self-employment rate (or a minority earnings measure) that is less than or equal to 80 percent of the corresponding non-minority measure. The distinction between these two types of "significance" has sometimes been a source of confusion to jurists (Gastwirth 1988, 248) and has, apparently, often been lost entirely by economists.[45]

A similar pattern of disparity is evident when only the full-time year-round subset is considered. In Table 2.10, the estimated self-employment rate for non-Hispanic whites is 14.7 percent—almost 2.5 times the black rate, 1.7 times the Hispanic rate, and 1.4 times the Native American rate. Except for Asians, each of these differences satisfies the 80 percent rule outlined above. Minority self-employment rates are each less than four-fifths of the non-Hispanic white rate and these differences are each statistically significantly different from zero at better than a one percent level. A comparison of Table 2.10 with Table 2.9 reveals that, except for Asians, self-employment rates are lower among the full-time employed than the part-time employed.

A final point to notice about Table 2.9 and Table 2.10 is the precision of the estimates across racial and ethnic groups. For example, the confidence intervals in Table 2.10 for black and Hispanic self-employment rates are more than twice as wide as that for non-Hispanic whites. For Asians they are five times wider, and for Native Americans they are almost thirteen times wider. These differences are driven, of course, by the relatively smaller sample sizes for minority groups compared to non-Hispanic whites—especially Asians, Native Americans, and "other" races.

Self-employment Earnings by Race and Hispanic Origin

Several well-known problems exist which affect the measurement of all types of labor market earnings, not just those of the self-employed. One of the most important is that aggregation across educational and age groups can mask underlying differences. I account for this possibility in the next chapter, where multiple correlation and regression analyses are employed to allow earnings comparisons that account for these differences.

Measured earnings may also include returns to physical capital in addition to labor. Although this holds for both wage and salary workers and the self-employed, one expects that the returns to capital should be, on average, more important to the latter group. Furthermore, measured earnings are net of non-wage forms of labor compensation such as paid time-off, insurance benefits, or pension benefits. This is true for the self-employed as well as for wage and salary workers.

An additional measurement issue is the underreporting of self-employment income to reduce tax liability. According to Aronson (1991, 141):

> Estimates of unreported income . . . range widely. . . There are no acceptable data that would permit a reliable adjustment of reported earnings, though one study found that the discrepancy between reported and actual earnings decreased with level of income or earnings. It is clear, however, that the self-employed have the largest propensity and best opportunity for underreporting taxable income. [The IRS] esti-

mated that only 60 to 65 percent of all self-employment income was reported in 1981 [citations omitted].

This is likely to be a larger problem in the data sources which rely directly on tax records, such as the IRS and the SSA data, than in sample survey-based data such as the CPS and the PUMS. In a 1981 study, for example, the U. S. General Accounting Office matched IRS and SSA records to CPS panelists and found that 16 percent of persons reporting as self-employed in the CPS did not report any taxable self-employment income to the IRS (Aronson 1991, 142).

Tables 2.11 and 2.12 present estimated average annual earnings by race and Hispanic origin, for both the self-employed and for wage and salary workers. As with self-employment rates, sizable earnings disparities are evident in both tables for all minority groups except Asians. In Table 2.11, average annual earnings for black and Native American business owners are slightly less than 60 percent of earnings for non-Hispanic white business owners. For Hispanics the ratio is about 66 percent. Each of these disparities is not only substantial but is also statistically significant at better than a one percent level. For Asian business owners, in contrast, average annual earnings are about 1.6 percent higher than earnings for non-Hispanic white business owners. This difference, however, is not statistically significant ($p = 0.221$).

Table 2.12 also shows a pattern of racial and ethnic disparity among the full-time self-employed. Average annual earnings for self-employed black, Hispanic, and Native Americans are estimated to be 66 percent, 69 percent, and 64 percent of non-Hispanic white self-employment earnings, respectively. Each of these differences is highly statistically significant ($p < 0.001$). The estimate of mean annual self-employment earnings for Asians, on the other hand, is essentially equal to that for whites and the difference between them is not statistically significant ($p = 0.838$). Estimated mean self-employment earnings for "other" races *is* statistically significantly different from that of whites ($p = 0.030$), and comes close to the threshold for substantiality ($\$41,754 \div \$50,744 = 0.823$).

Tables 2.11 and 2.12 also include estimates of the standard deviation of annual earnings for the self-employed versus wage and salary workers by race and Hispanic origin. Consistent with classical Knightian ideas of entrepreneurship, in which entrepreneurs bear risk but also claim profits, the dispersion in the earnings of the self-employed is much greater than for wage and salary workers. This is true regardless of race or Hispanic origin, although the differences are even more pronounced for minorities

Table 2.11. Estimated average annual earnings for the self-employed and for wage and salary workers, by race and Hispanic origin, 1989

Class of Worker and Race/Ethnic Group	Average Annual Earnings	Confidence Interval (Lower 95%)	Confidence Interval (Upper 95%)	Standard Deviation
All Employed (1):				
Self-employed	$44,043	$43,842	$44,245	$47,991
Wage and salary	32,217	32,171	32,263	27,432
Self-employed:				
NH white	45,698	45,479	45,917	48,683
NH black	27,082	26,280	27,884	34,515
Hispanic	29,960	29,275	30,644	37,156
NH Asian	46,438	45,274	47,602	52,244
NH Native Amer.	26,954	24,575	29,333	33,828
NH other race	35,623	28,738	42,507	44,609
Wage and Salary:				
NH white	34,897	34,842	34,951	28,784
NH black	21,574	21,471	21,677	16,640
Hispanic	20,749	20,650	20,847	16,754
NH Asian	30,219	29,950	30,488	27,268
NH Native Amer.	22,767	22,291	23,242	18,264
NH other race	23,469	22,563	24,374	16,448

Source: Author's calculations from Bureau of the Census (1993).
Notes: (1) Includes males, age 25–64, employed for pay in 1989, residing in metropolitan areas, working in the for-profit, private, nonagricultural sector. Numbers may not add to total due to rounding; (2) "NH" stands for "Non-Hispanic"; (3) Hispanics can be of any race; (4) Sample size and population size in each category are the same as in Tables 2.7 and 2.9.

than for non-minorities. Only one other study that I am aware of has made this observation (Borjas and Bronars 1989, 602).

Another striking aspect of Tables 2.11 and 2.12 is that estimated earnings are substantially higher for the self-employed than for wage and salary workers. This is true overall and also when considered according

Table 2.12. Estimated average annual earnings for the self-employed and for wage and salary workers, by race and Hispanic origin, 1989 (full-time, year-round only)

Class of Worker and Race/Ethnic Group	Average Annual Earnings	Confidence Interval (Lower 95%)	Confidence Interval (Upper 95%)	Standard Deviation
All Employed (1):				
Self-employed	$49,316	$49,084	$49,549	$53,349
Wage and salary	35,576	35,526	35,627	29,248
Self-employed:				
NH white	50,744	50,494	50,994	53,917
NH black	33,555	32,468	34,643	41,171
Hispanic	34,922	34,069	35,776	42,924
NH Asian	50,605	49,288	51,922	57,483
NH Native Amer.	32,374	29,326	35,422	39,292
NH other race	41,754	33,620	49,888	49,104
Wage and Salary:				
NH white	37,969	37,910	38,029	30,672
NH black	25,240	25,126	25,355	17,317
Hispanic	23,638	23,528	23,749	17,828
NH Asian	34,150	33,846	34,455	29,728
NH Native Amer.	27,129	26,600	27,658	19,454
NH other race	26,660	25,692	27,627	17,016

Source: Author's calculations from Bureau of the Census (1993).
Notes: (1) Includes males, age 25–64, employed for pay in 1989, residing in metropolitan areas, working in the for-profit, private, nonagricultural sector for 35 hours or more per week and for 40 or more weeks per year. Numbers may not add to total due to rounding; (2) "NH" stands for "Non-Hispanic"; (3) Hispanics can be of any race; (4) Sample size and population size in each category are the same as in Tables 2.8 and 2.10.

to race and Hispanic origin. It is also true regardless of the inclusion of the part-time employed in the sample. The typical full-time, year-round self-employed male, for example, earned $49,316 in 1989 compared to $35,576 for the typical wage and salary worker—almost forty percent more. This earnings advantage is most pronounced for minority groups, especially Hispanics and Asians.

This finding contrasts sharply with most other studies of self-employment, which have found a substantial earnings *disadvantage* to being self-employed. Aronson (1991, 46–47) reports that "[a]ll but a few post-World War II studies of self-employment report that the earnings of the self-employed are, on average, less than those of individuals who are employed by others." The difference in Table 2.11 and 2.12 is not inconsistent, however, with these previous findings. Rather it is probably due to the inclusion of the incorporated self-employed along with the unincorporated self-employed. All the studies cited by Aronson are based on data sources—CPS data, IRS data, and Survey of Income and Program Participation (SIPP) data—that classify the incorporated self-employed as wage and salary workers rather than as self-employed. The incorporated self-employed tend to have higher earnings than the unincorporated self-employed. As Aronson himself notes (1991, 43), "[t]he earnings of [the incorporated self-employed] are distinctly greater, on average, than the earnings of the unincorporated self-employed. Most studies ignore this difference, however, because the overall effect on earnings comparisons is likely to be quite small."

Aronson's conclusion that the effect on earnings comparisons of counting the incorporated as self-employed is "likely to be quite small" seems to be based on his belief that incorporated businesses are only a very small proportion of all business enterprises, and that consequently even large differences in earnings between the incorporated and the unincorporated could not have much of an effect on overall comparisons. In contrast to Aronson, I find that substantial numbers of the self-employed are incorporated and that their inclusion or exclusion from the definition of self-employed has a large impact on earnings comparisons with wage and salary workers.

As the results presented in Table 2.7 through Table 2.12 demonstrate, the PUMS dataset prepared for this study yields conclusions consistent with the national, economy-wide, conclusions on racial and ethnic differences in self-employment rates and earnings extant in the literature and discussed in chapter one. Particularly, relative to non-Hispanic whites, disparities in self-employment rates for blacks, Hispanics, and Native Americans are statistically and substantively significant. Although statistically significant, self-employment rates for Asians— at least when combined together into one broad racial category—are often not substantively significant and, in some cases, are higher than corresponding rates for non-Hispanic whites. In the next section, the focus shifts to see if these findings are robust to geographic disaggregation.

ESTIMATES OF DISAGGREGATED DISPARITIES IN RACIAL AND ETHNIC SELF-EMPLOYMENT RATES AND EARNINGS

One of the principal questions that I wish to examine in this study is whether or not the racial and ethnic disparities in self-employment rates and earnings at the national and economy-wide level persist or disappear when different parts of the country or different sectors of the industrial or occupational distribution are examined.[46] If there are different proportions of minorities across these various subgroups, and if different subgroups possess different propensities toward self-employment, then it is possible that aggregate statistics could show disparities even when virtually all subgroups show no disparity. This effect is sometimes referred to as "Simpson's paradox," and it has been used by several commentators to cast doubt on existence of racial and ethnic discrimination in business enterprise (*e.g.* La Noue 1994b). Meier, Sacks, and Zabell (1986, 18) recount an example of Simpson's paradox concerning graduate school admissions for men and women at the University of California at Berkeley.

> Overall, the percentage of male applicants admitted in 1973 was significantly *higher* than the percentage of female applicants admitted, but a survey of the admissions to individual departments showed that for virtually all departments the admission rate for male applicants was *lower* than the admission rate for females.
>
> This paradoxical situation, sometimes referred to as *Simpson's paradox*, actually has a very simple explanation. At Berkeley, women had applied preferentially to departments such as English and history, with large numbers of applicants and corresponding low rates of admission, while men had applied preferentially to departments such as mathematics and physics, with fewer applicants and hence much higher rates of admission. Simpson's paradox should not be thought of as a rare or freakish event: other instances can easily be found.

It is important that Simpson's paradox be considered in the present context because there is evidence that the geographic distribution of various minority groups is substantially different from that of non-minorities. Furthermore, it will be demonstrated below that there are large differences in self-employment rates across industries. Insofar as minority groups are disproportionately concentrated in industries or occupations with low rates of self-employment, this factor alone *could* account for differences observed at the aggregate level. On the other hand, if a pattern of disparity still emerges when various industrial and occupational subgroups are considered separately, this would be evidence against Simpson's paradox and for the discrimination hypothesis. It is also likely that, given the number of geographic and industry subgroups being considered, a mixture of both phenomena will be observed.

I will examine two summary levels of geography in this section: region and division. The Census Bureau classifies the United States into four regions and nine divisions. They are organized as follows:

I.   Northeast Region
   A.   New England Division
      1.   Connecticut
      2.   Maine
      3.   Massachusetts
      4.   New Hampshire
      5.   Rhode Island
      6.   Vermont
   B.   Middle Atlantic Division
      1.   New Jersey
      2.   New York
      3.   Pennsylvania

II.   Midwest Region
   A.   East North Central Division
      1.   Illinois
      2.   Indiana
      3.   Michigan
      4.   Ohio
      5.   Wisconsin
   B.   West North Central Division
      1.   Iowa
      2.   Kansas
      3.   Minnesota
      4.   Missouri
      5.   Nebraska
      6.   North Dakota
      7.   South Dakota

III.   South Region
   A.   South Atlantic Division
      1.   Delaware
      2.   District of Columbia
      3.   Florida
      4.   Georgia
      5.   Maryland
      6.   North Carolina
      7.   South Carolina
      8.   Virginia
      9.   West Virginia
   B.   East South Central Division
      1.   Alabama
      2.   Kentucky
      3.   Mississippi
      4.   Tennessee
   C.   West South Central Division
      1.   Arkansas
      2.   Louisiana
      3.   Texas
      4.   Oklahoma

IV.   West Region
   A.   Mountain Division
      1.   Arizona
      2.   Colorado
      3.   Idaho
      4.   Montana
      5.   Nevada
      6.   New Mexico
      7.   Utah
      8.   Wyoming
   B.   Pacific Division
      1.   Alaska
      2.   California
      3.   Hawaii
      4.   Oregon
      5.   Washington

Estimates Disaggregated by Region

The United States is a vast country with an enormous amount of physical, historical, economic, and cultural diversity. The size of minority populations differs from region to region, as does their industrial and occupational distribution. In theory such differences, if they are substantial, are capable of accounting for the disparities documented in this chapter. In this section I examine self-employment rates and earnings by region to determine if these regional differences can explain the observed racial and ethnic disparities.

Nonagricultural self-employment rates in the Northeast (14.2 percent), South (14.0 percent), and West (15.0 percent) are all much higher than the rate in the Midwest (11.2 percent). These estimates are all quite precise. The spread of each 95 percent confidence interval is less than 0.5 percent. Approximately 24 percent of the sample lives in the Northeast, 32 percent in the South, 23 percent in the Midwest, and 21 percent in the West.

The higher estimated average annual earnings of the self-employed relative to wage and salary workers at the national level persists when the data are disaggregated by region. Average annual earnings of the self-employed in the Northeast ($52,127) and the West ($51,683) both exceed the national average of $49,316 reported in Table 2.12. Self-employment earnings in the Midwest ($49,043) were approximately equal to the national average. Mean earnings of the self-employed in the South ($45,614) are about 8 percent lower than the national average and about 13 percent lower than the Northeast, but are still substantially in excess of annual earnings for their Southern wage and salary counterparts. All four estimates are very precise. Standard errors range between approximately $200 and $300 dollars—less than one percent of estimated earnings levels.

Self-employment rates by race and Hispanic origin. Table 2.13 shows that Non-Hispanic white self-employment rates substantially exceed black, Hispanic, and Native American self-employment rates in all four regions of the country. The highest ratio of black to white self-employment rates is 47 percent in the West. The lowest ratio is 38 percent in the South. Hispanic to white ratios are also very low except in the South. The ratio varies from 42 percent in the Midwest to 45 percent in the West and 55 percent in the Northeast. In the South, however, the ratio is 78 percent. Similar to Hispanics, the ratio of Native American self-

Table 2.13. Estimated self-employment rate and self-employed population, by census region, and by race and Hispanic origin, 1990

Geographic Region	Race/Ethnic Group	Self-Employment Rate	Confidence Interval (Lower 95%)	Confidence Interval (Upper 95%)	Self Employed Population
Northeast	NH White	15.2	15.1	15.3	906,543
	Black	6.5	6.1	6.9	29,678
	Hispanic	8.3	7.8	8.7	35,143
	Asian	16.4	15.6	17.2	34,653
	Native	7.3	5.0	9.7	719
	Other	6.6	3.9	9.2	505
South	NH White	15.3	15.2	15.4	1,154,642
	Black	5.8	5.5	6.0	64,028
	Hispanic	11.9	11.5	12.2	85,694
	Asian	18.0	17.0	19.1	26,148
	Native	12.7	11.2	14.3	5,884
	Other	10.5	6.3	14.8	579
Midwest	NH White	11.9	11.8	12.0	762,119
	Black	4.7	4.3	5.0	20,822
	Hispanic	5.0	4.5	5.5	10,088
	Asian	15.8	14.5	17.1	14,874
	Native	8.2	6.3	10.1	1,751
	Other	9.9	3.4	16.4	209
West	NH White	17.0	16.8	17.1	803,394
	Black	8.0	7.5	8.6	19,210
	Hispanic	7.6	7.4	7.9	80,140
	Asian	15.6	15.1	16.1	80,093
	Native	10.0	8.6	11.5	4,090
	Other	11.9	9.2	14.7	1,789

Source: Author's calculations from Bureau of the Census (1993).

Notes: (1) Includes males, age 25–64, employed for pay in 1989, residing in metropolitan areas, working full-time and year-round in the for-profit, private, nonagricultural sector. Numbers may not add to total due to rounding; (2) "NH" stands for "Non-Hispanic"; (3) Hispanics can be of any race.

employment rates to white rates is very low in all but the Southern region, where it is slightly higher than the 80 percent substantiality threshold. Except for "other races" in the Midwest region, all of these differences are statistically significant at better than a 0.005 level. Consequently, the 80 percent rule is met for blacks and Hispanics in all four regions, for Native Americans in all regions but the South, and for "other races" in all regions but the Midwest. Asian self-employment rates, on the other hand, exceed non-Hispanic white rates in all regions but the West. Interestingly, the West is the region of the country where the Asian population is most numerous. These differences are all statistically significant but, except for the Midwest, none of them are very large. The Asian self-employment rate in the Midwest is 15.8 percent, compared with a white rate of only 11.9 percent. Ninety-five percent confidence intervals for these data are also provided. The confidence intervals are fairly narrow for the white, black, Hispanic, and Asian estimates, but are quite wide for the Native American and "other race" estimates.

Self-employment earnings by race and Hispanic origin. Table 2.14 provides estimated average annual self-employment earnings by race and Hispanic origin in each region of the U.S. These earnings estimates are reasonably precise for all but the Native American and "other race" minority groups. Black, Hispanic, and Native American self-employment earnings are significantly less than non-Hispanic white earnings in every instance. All of these differences are highly statistically significant ($p < 0.001$), and the minority-to-non-minority earnings ratio is less than 80 percent in each case except for the relatively small population of Hispanics in the Midwest region, for whom the ratio is slightly higher (0.82) than the 80 percent threshold.

Asians are again the exception to this general pattern, registering higher average self-employment earnings in the South and the Midwest and lower earnings in the Northeast and the West. The differences in the Northeast, the South, and the West, although all statistically significantly different from zero, are all relatively small. The exception is the Midwest region, where estimated average earnings for Asians are almost 38 percent higher than their non-minority counterparts. This difference is statistically significant at better than a five percent level.

This examination of self-employment rates and earnings by region confirms—with very few exceptions—the existence of large and statistically significant disparities in all regions of the United States and for all minority groups except Asians.

Table 2.14. Estimated average annual earnings of the self-employed and of wage and salary workers, by census region, and by race and Hispanic origin, 1990

Geographic Region	Race/Ethnic Group	Self-Employment Earnings	Confidence Interval (Lower 95%)	Confidence Interval (Upper 95%)	Wages and Salary Worker Earnings
Northeast	NH White	$53,550	$53,048	$54,052	$40,878
	Black	35,046	32,716	37,376	27,237
	Hispanic	33,191	31,376	35,006	24,909
	Asian	49,450	46,573	52,326	35,971
	Native	33,291	24,036	42,546	29,902
	Other	29,949	22,301	37,597	24,680
South	NH White	47,307	46,877	47,737	35,435
	Black	29,497	28,164	30,835	22,502
	Hispanic	34,094	32,728	35,464	22,454
	Asian	51,738	48,197	55,286	32,301
	Native	30,036	25,667	34,409	25,760
	Other	37,755	17,233	58,277	23,147
Midwest	NH White	49,189	48,623	49,754	36,563
	Black	36,017	32,872	39,163	27,684
	Hispanic	40,575	35,802	45,348	24,989
	Asian	67,645	61,898	73,392	37,375
	Native	29,489	21,675	37,303	27,121
	Other	63,499	19,603	107,395	30,877
West	NH White	53,994	53,463	54,525	40,364
	Black	42,110	38,643	45,577	29,626
	Hispanic	35,856	34,471	37,240	23,637
	Asian	47,571	45,993	49,148	33,324
	Native	36,811	31,108	42,514	27,950
	Other	43,840	33,055	54,626	28,434

Source: Author's calculations from Bureau of the Census (1993).
Notes: (1) Includes males, age 25–64, employed for pay in 1989, residing in metropolitan areas, working full-time and year-round in the for-profit, private, nonagricultural sector. Numbers may not add to total due to rounding; (2) "NH" stands for "Non-Hispanic"; (3) Hispanics can be of any race.

Estimates Disaggregated by Census Division

Table 2.15 presents estimated self-employment rates by race and Hispanic origin for the nine Census geographic divisions, and includes the corresponding ninety-five percent confidence intervals for these rates.[47] It is immediately apparent from this table that the pattern of racial disparity in self-employment rates observed at the national level and at the regional level persists at the census division level as well.

Black self-employment rates in the full-time, year-round sample are substantially lower than non-Hispanic white rates in all nine geographic divisions. Black self-employment rates range between 4.6 and 6.6 percent in eight of nine divisions. In the Pacific states the rate is 8.5 percent. The highest black self-employment rate in any division is lower by almost three percentage points than the lowest non-Hispanic white self-employment rate. The disparity between black rates and white rates meets the 80 percent test in all nine divisions. In each instance the p-value is less than 0.001. The ratio of black to white self-employment rates in each division ranges between 34 and 49 percent.

Hispanic self-employment rates are also generally very low relative to non-Hispanic white rates. Exceptions are the South Atlantic and East South Central divisions, where Hispanic self-employment rates are within about one percentage point of non-Hispanic whites. The Hispanic self-employment rate actually exceeds the non-Hispanic white rate in the East South Central division—15.2 percent versus 13.9 percent. These differences, however, are not statistically significant. Hispanic self-employment rates in the other seven divisions are all lower than the lowest non-Hispanic white rate. The disparity between Hispanic rates and white rates meets both prongs of the 80 percent test in all seven of these divisions. In those divisions where the test is met, the ratio of Hispanic to white self-employment rates ranges between 37 and 61 percent.

Native American self-employment rates are below non-Hispanic white rates in all nine divisions. As with Hispanics, the differences in the East South Central and the South Atlantic states, however, are marginal in size and not statistically significant. The lowest rate of self-employment for Native Americans is 5.1 percent in the New England states, while the highest rate is 14.4 percent in the South Atlantic states.

The exceptional nature of Asian self-employment also appears to be fairly robust to disaggregation by geographic division. Asian self-employment rates range between 11.6 percent in the New England states and 19.5 percent in the South Atlantic states—substantially higher than for other minority groups. Asian self-employment rates exceed non-Hispanic white rates in six of nine divisions. In only three of these cases, however, are these differences statistically significant—in the Mid Atlantic division, the East North Central division, and the South Atlantic division. There is only one division, New England, where Asian self-employment rates are statistically significant and less than 80 percent of non-Hispanic white rates.

To indicate the degree of precision in these estimated rates, Table 2.15 also includes 95 percent confidence intervals. The estimates of self-employment for non-Hispanic whites are quite precise at this level of geographic disaggregation. The spread of the confidence intervals for non-Hispanic whites ranges between 0.3 percent and 0.7 percent. Estimated self-employment rates for blacks are somewhat less precise than those for non-Hispanic whites. The spread of the confidence interval for blacks ranges from 0.6 percent in the South Atlantic states (where black populations are relatively large) to 2.6 percent in the Mountain states (where black populations are relatively small).

Confidence intervals for Hispanic self-employment rates are similar to those for blacks except for two divisions—the West North Central and East South Central—in which they are quite wide. Not surprisingly, both of these divisions have very small Hispanic populations. Similar patterns are evident for the other groups as well. The spread in the confidence intervals for Asians ranges from one percentage point in the Pacific states, where Asians are relatively numerous, to almost nine percentage points in the East South Central states, where they are not. The spread for Native Americans is between three and four percentage points in the Pacific and the West South Central states where they are most numerous, and varies between five and seven percentage points in most other divisions. In the East South Central states, where Native Americans are least populous, the spread is almost 14 percentage points.

A comparison of Tables 2.13 and 2.15 highlights the importance of aggregation issues in measuring disparities. Hispanic self-employment rates in the South were found to be statistically significant and less than 80 percent of corresponding rates for non-Hispanic whites. When the South is disaggregated into its three component divisions, however, a somewhat different picture emerges. In the West South Central division, Hispanic self-employment rates are only about 61 percent of white rates. In the South Atlantic division, the rates are almost equal (15.1 versus 15.4 percent, respectively). In the East South Central division, however, Hispanic rates are higher than corresponding white rates. Despite this,

Table 2.15. Estimated self-employment rate and self-employed population, by census division, and by race and Hispanic origin, 1990

Geographic Division	Race/Ethnic Group	Self-Employment Rate (%)	Confidence Interval (Lower 95%)	Confidence Interval (Upper 95%)	Self-Employed Population
New England	NH White	15.0	14.7	15.2	260,735
	Black	5.4	4.5	6.4	3,325
	Hispanic	5.5	4.5	6.5	3,092
	Asian	11.6	9.7	13.4	3,699
	Native	5.1	1.6	8.6	140
Mid Atlantic	NH White	15.3	15.1	15.5	645,808
	Black	6.6	6.2	7.1	26,353
	Hispanic	8.7	8.2	9.2	32,051
	Asian	17.3	16.3	18.2	30,954
	Native	8.2	5.2	11.2	579
E. N. Central	NH White	11.5	11.3	11.6	542,672
	Black	4.6	4.3	5.0	17,514
	Hispanic	4.7	4.1	5.2	8,359
	Asian	16.4	14.9	17.8	12,751
	Native	7.1	4.9	9.4	914
W. N. Central	NH White	13.0	12.8	13.3	219,447
	Black	4.8	3.9	5.7	3,308
	Hispanic	7.4	5.4	9.3	1,729
	Asian	13.1	10.1	16.1	2,123
	Native	9.8	6.5	13.1	837
S. Atlantic	NH White	15.4	15.3	15.6	627,638
	Black	6.1	5.8	6.4	40,971
	Hispanic	15.1	14.4	15.7	42,621
	Asian	19.5	18.1	20.9	15,806
	Native	14.4	11.5	17.2	2,051
E. S. Central	NH White	13.9	13.6	14.2	167,025
	Black	4.7	4.1	5.2	7,778
	Hispanic	15.2	10.8	19.5	997
	Asian	17.0	12.6	21.3	1,280
	Native	13.1	6.2	19.9	411

Geographic Division	Race/Ethnic Group	Self-Employment Rate (%)	Confidence Interval (Lower 95%)	Confidence Interval (Upper 95%)	Self-Employed Population
W. S. Central	NH White	15.8	15.6	16.0	359,979
	Black	5.6	5.1	6.1	15,279
	Hispanic	9.7	9.2	10.1	42,076
	Asian	16.1	14.5	17.6	9,062
	Native	11.9	10.0	13.8	3,422
Mountain	NH White	15.3	15.0	15.7	175,908
	Black	5.3	4.0	6.6	1,781
	Hispanic	7.9	7.2	8.6	11,237
	Asian	13.4	11.1	15.7	3,091
	Native	7.6	5.0	10.3	785
Pacific	NH White	17.5	17.3	17.7	627,486
	Black	8.5	7.8	9.1	17,429
	Hispanic	7.6	7.3	7.9	68,903
	Asian	15.7	15.2	16.2	77,002
	Native	10.8	9.2	12.5	3,305

Source: Author's calculations from Bureau of the Census (1993).
Notes: (1) Includes males, age 25–64, employed for pay in 1989, residing in metropolitan areas, working full-time and year-round in the for-profit, private, nonagricultural sector. Numbers may not add to total due to rounding; (2) "NH" stands for "Non-Hispanic"; (3) Hispanics can be of any race.

when considering the South as a whole, the overall results clearly show disparity because: (a) the differences in the South Atlantic and East South Central divisions are neither large nor statistically significant, (b) the differences in the West South Central are large and highly statistically significant, and (c) the bulk of the Hispanics in the sample—60 percent—reside in the West South Central division.

Table 2.16 presents self-employment earnings estimates by census division for each race and Hispanic origin group in the sample. For blacks, the 80 percent rule for statistically significant and substantive disparity is met in all nine divisions. The ratio of black to white self-employment earnings ranges between 57 percent in the Mountain division to 80 percent in the West North Central division.

For Hispanics, the 80 percent rule is met in five of nine divisions (Middle Atlantic, South Atlantic, West South Central, Mountain, and Pacific). In

Table 2.16. Estimated average annual earnings of the self-employed and of wage and salary workers, by census division, and by race and Hispanic origin, 1990

Geographic Division	Race/ Ethnic Group	Self- Employment Rate (%)	Confidence Interval (Lower 95%)	Confidence Interval (Upper 95%)	Self- Employed Population
New England	NH White	$50,847	$49,996	$51,698	40,648
	Black	37,471	30,797	44,144	28,206
	Hispanic	42,408	35,511	49,305	24,939
	Asian	59,017	49,484	68,551	36,001
	Native	42,787	21,999	63,575	29,364
Mid Atlantic	NH White	54,642	54,027	55,256	40,974
	Black	34,740	32,256	37,224	27,087
	Hispanic	32,302	30,435	34,169	24,904
	Asian	48,306	45,302	51,310	35,965
	Native	30,995	20,700	41,290	30,120
E. N. Central	NH White	50,639	49,969	51,310	37,226
	Black	35,894	32,458	39,329	28,159
	Hispanic	41,548	36,252	46,843	24,776
	Asian	68,363	62,342	74,384	38,658
	Native	30,974	19,521	42,427	28,837
W. N. Central	NH White	45,602	44,551	46,653	34,664
	Black	36,673	28,855	44,490	25,075
	Hispanic	35,874	24,863	46,886	26,672
	Asian	63,332	45,645	81,020	31,430
	Native	27,867	17,320	38,413	24,468
S. Atlantic	NH White	48,226	47,647	48,805	35,645
	Black	30,482	28,882	32,081	22,716
	Hispanic	36,872	34,983	38,762	24,886
	Asian	55,033	50,434	59,632	32,292
	Native	32,063	23,937	40,189	26,471
E. S. Central	NH White	45,700	44,547	46,853	32,381
	Black	27,173	22,489	31,856	20,796
	Hispanic	41,660	27,340	55,980	30,545
	Asian	50,812	37,203	64,421	36,709
	Native	25,229	13,538	36,919	28,247

Geographic Division	Race/ Ethnic Group	Self- Employment Rate (%)	Confidence Interval (Lower 95%)	Confidence Interval (Upper 95%)	Self- Employed Population
W. S. Central	NH White	46,451	45,679	47,222	36,704
	Black	28,042	25,332	30,751	23,030
	Hispanic	31,100	29,104	33,097	20,852
	Asian	46,123	40,097	52,150	31,729
	Native	29,399	23,849	34,948	25,147
Mountain	NH White	44,739	43,721	45,757	34,883
	Black	25,429	20,753	30,106	24,160
	Hispanic	33,778	30,034	37,522	22,104
	Asian	37,021	30,009	44,034	28,592
	Native	27,671	18,993	36,348	22,223
Pacific	NH White	56,589	55,975	57,203	42,162
	Black	43,815	40,054	47,575	30,549
	Hispanic	36,194	34,705	37,684	23,876
	Asian	47,994	46,377	49,611	33,553
	Native	38,982	32,296	45,668	29,953

Source: Author's calculations from Bureau of the Census (1993).
Notes: (1) Includes males, age 25–64, employed for pay in 1989, residing in metropolitan areas, working full-time and year-round in the for-profit, private, nonagricultural sector; Numbers may not add to total due to rounding; (2) "NH" stands for "Non-Hispanic"; (3) Hispanics can be of any race.

these divisions, earnings ratios range between 59 percent in the Middle Atlantic states to 79 percent in the West North Central states. Differences for Hispanics are statistically significant and just over the 80 percent threshold in two other divisions (New England and East North Central). In the remaining two divisions the differences are not statistically significant.

For Native Americans, the 80 percent rule is met in eight of the nine divisions. The exception is in New England, where the difference is not statistically significantly different from zero. Earnings ratios for Native Americans range between 55 percent in the East South Central states and 69 percent in the Pacific states.

Estimates Disaggregated by Industry Division

Evidence from the 1992 SMOBE. Before continuing with the analysis of the PUMS sample, Tables 2.17 and 2.18 present statistics from the 1992 SMOBE according to an industry division scheme that is very similar to that used in the PUMS. Table 2.17 shows the percentage of firms owned by minorities in each industry division in 1992. It also shows the percentage of annual aggregate sales and receipts earned by minority-owned firms in each division. As with the all industry statistics presented above (*see* Table 1.2), the market share of minority-owned businesses is far lower than expected based on availability. For example, although minority firms constitute 9.1 percent of all firms in the construction division, these firms earned only 5.1 percent of construction sales and receipts.

Table 2.17 shows large disparities in all industrial divisions except mining (column C). Minority market share is never more than about two-thirds of minority availability. The largest disparity ratios occur in transportation, manufacturing, retail trade, construction, and wholesale trade. However, there does not appear to be any clear association between the size of the disparity (column C) and the level of availability (column A) or of market share (column B).

Table 2.17. Minority firm population shares and market shares, by industry division, 1987 and 1992

Industry Division	Minority Firms as a Percentage of All U.S. firms	Minority Receipts as a Percentage of All U.S. Receipts	Disparity Index — Column (B) as a Percentage of Column (A)
	(A)	(B)	(C)
All industries	11.4	6.1	53.3
Agric. services, forestry & fishing	12.7	8.5	67.1
Mining	1.9	2.6	136.1
Construction	9.1	5.1	56.5
Manufacturing	9.1	3.5	38.1
Transport, comm. & public utilities	17.0	6.4	37.6
Wholesale trade	8.3	5.2	62.5
Retail trade	13.0	7.3	56.0
Finance, insurance & real estate	7.8	5.4	68.6
Services	12.0	8.0	66.2
Industries not classified	13.4	10.9	81.4

Source: Author's calculations from Bureau of the Census (1996e).

Table 2.17 also shows that minority firms are relatively overrepresented in the transportation, retail, services, and agricultural services sectors and relatively underrepresented in mining, finance, wholesale trade, manufacturing, and construction. It appears from the table that minority market share tends to be higher in industry sectors with more minority availability. Market share is largest in agricultural services, services, retail, and transportation. It is smallest in mining, manufacturing, construction, wholesale trade, and finance. More formal tests confirm this impression. The simple Pearson correlation between column (A) and column (B) of 0.72 is positive, large, and statistically significant. Spearman's *rho*, which is less sensitive to extreme values, is 0.73 and is also statistically significant.

Table 2.18 presents a supplemental view of these disparities in terms of average annual receipts per firm. Visual inspection appears to show that the size distribution of firms across industry divisions (according to

Table 2.18. Average annual minority and non-minority sales and receipts per firm

Industry Division	Annual Receipts Per Firm— All U.S. Firms	Annual Receipts Per Firm— Minority Firms	Disparity Index — Column (B) as a Percent of Column (A)
	(A)	(B)	(C)
All industries	$192,672	$102,775	53.3
Agric. services, forestry & fishing	68,529	46,012	67.1
Mining	217,207	295,680	136.1
Construction	167,862	94,898	56.5
Manufacturing	872,526	332,430	38.1
Transport, comm. & public utilities	186,053	69,977	37.6
Wholesale trade	1,190,794	744,520	62.5
Retail trade	291,646	163,236	56.0
Finance, insurance & real estate	166,021	113,810	68.6
Services	84,954	56,269	66.2
Industries not classified	29,130	23,709	81.4

Source: Author's calculations from Bureau of the Census (1996e).

sales and receipts) is similar for minority firms and non-minority firms. That is, firms in wholesale trade and manufacturing tend to be largest; firms in retail, mining, transportation, construction, and finance occupy the middle range; and services and agricultural services firms are smallest. Again, the visual impression is confirmed by more formal tests. The standard Pearson correlation between column (B) and column (C) is 0.93 and highly statistically significant. Spearman's *rho* is 0.94 and is highly statistically significant. Despite the large disparities between minority and non-minority firms, there are obviously commonalities as well.

There is some weak evidence in Table 2.18 that the disparities are larger in industry divisions with larger average firm size. The Pearson correlation between column (A) and column (C) is -0.26 but is not statistically significant. The Spearman test also cannot reject the hypothesis of independence between column (A) and column (C), or between column (B) and column (C).

As the reader can see, although the underlying populations are defined differently, the pattern of racial and ethnic disparity in the 1992 SMOBE statistics is quite similar to the that which is found in the 1990 PUMS.

Self-employment rates. Turning back now to the PUMS, Tables 2.19 and 2.20 present estimated self-employment rates and earnings by industry division from the PUMS sample. As with the SMOBE data, the economy-wide pattern of disparities in self-employment rates for blacks, Hispanics, and Native Americans tends to persist when the PUMS data are disaggregated to the industry division level, as in Table 2.19. Self-employment rates for non-Hispanic whites exceed those of blacks in every industry division examined. The 80 percent rule is satisfied for blacks in ten of these eleven cases. The exception is the transportation, communications, and public utilities (TCPU) sector. There, black rates are essentially equal to those of non-Hispanic whites. Black self-employment rate ratios are extremely low in manufacturing (0.24), mining (0.25), wholesale trade (0.26), retail trade (0.32), and professional services (0.33). In all but the entertainment services division, where the ratio is 0.50, black self-employment rates are less than half the corresponding white rate.

Non-Hispanic white self-employment rates exceed Hispanic rates in ten of eleven industry divisions. In the TCPU division, however, Hispanic rates are substantially in excess of and statistically significantly different from white rates. In all ten instances the 80 percent rule is met for Hispanics.

Table 2.19. Estimated self-employment rate and self-employed population, by industry division, and by race and Hispanic origin, 1990

Industry Division	Race/Ethnic Group	Self-Employment Rate (%)	Confidence Interval (Lower 95%)	Confidence Interval (Upper 95%)	Self-Employed Population
Mining					
	NH White	6.3	5.8	6.7	16,282
	Black	1.6	0.5	2.7	218
	Hispanic	1.5	0.6	2.5	252
	Asian	1.6	0.0	3.8	49
	Native	8.9	2.3	15.5	178
Construction					
	NH White	24.9	24.7	25.2	725,899
	Black	12.2	11.5	13.0	24,995
	Hispanic	13.3	12.7	13.8	41,494
	Asian	16.4	14.8	18.0	8,567
	Native	18.7	15.9	21.4	3,552
Manufacturing					
	NH White	4.0	4.0	4.1	298,685
	Black	1.0	0.8	1.1	6,788
	Hispanic	2.5	2.3	2.6	18,061
	Asian	3.7	3.3	4.0	10,062
	Native	3.6	2.6	4.5	1,296
Transp., Comm. & Public Utils.					
	NH White	6.5	6.4	6.7	162,144
	Black	6.2	5.8	6.7	19,783
	Hispanic	8.1	7.5	8.7	16,578
	Asian	8.7	7.6	9.8	5,776
	Native	6.3	4.4	8.1	897
Wholesale Trade					
	NH White	11.1	10.9	11.3	225,371
	Black	2.9	2.4	3.4	4,190
	Hispanic	7.4	6.8	8.1	13,008
	Asian	14.9	13.5	16.2	9,795
	Native	6.1	3.7	8.5	483

Table 2.19. Estimated self-employment rate and self-employed population, by industry division, and by race and Hispanic origin, 1990 (*cont.*)

Industry Division	Race/Ethnic Group	Self-Employment Rate (%)	Confidence Interval (Lower 95%)	Confidence Interval (Upper 95%)	Self-Employed Population
Retail Trade					
	NH White	16.9	16.7	17.1	581,643
	Black	5.4	4.9	5.8	16,630
	Hispanic	10.0	9.5	10.4	41,967
	Asian	25.5	24.6	26.5	52,593
	Native	11.0	8.6	13.5	1,758
Finance, Insur. & Real Estate					
	NH White	18.1	17.8	18.4	327,840
	Black	7.3	6.6	8.1	9,679
	Hispanic	9.4	8.5	10.2	10,559
	Asian	13.8	12.6	15.1	9,985
	Native	11.9	7.1	16.8	593
Business Services					
	NH White	25.3	25.0	25.6	408,910
	Black	12.4	11.5	13.3	20,433
	Hispanic	16.9	16.0	17.8	31,635
	Asian	19.4	17.8	21.0	11,372
	Native	18.6	14.6	22.7	1,530
Personal Services					
	NH White	26.7	26.0	27.4	105,618
	Black	11.9	10.5	13.2	8,084
	Hispanic	11.3	10.2	12.4	9,201
	Asian	27.9	25.7	30.1	11,630
	Native	12.9	6.4	19.5	288
Entertainment Services					
	NH White	22.2	21.4	23.0	59,335
	Black	11.2	9.1	13.3	2,772
	Hispanic	10.4	8.7	12.1	3,127
	Asian	18.6	14.9	22.3	1,754
	Native	16.5	6.6	26.4	226

Industry Division	Race/Ethnic Group	Self-Employment Rate (%)	Confidence Interval (Lower 95%)	Confidence Interval (Upper 95%)	Self-Employed Population
Professional Services					
	NH White	35.0	34.7	35.3	714,971
	Black	11.6	10.8	12.4	20,166
	Hispanic	19.6	18.5	20.7	25,183
	Asian	29.7	28.4	31.0	34,185
	Native	28.5	22.7	34.4	1,643

Source: *Author's calculations from Bureau of the Census (1993).*

Native American self-employment rates fall below those of whites in ten of eleven instances. The 80 percent rule is satisfied in seven of these ten cases. Differences for Native Americans were not statistically significant in the remaining three divisions. Native American self-employment rates exceed those of whites in the mining division, but the difference is not statistically significant.

The Asian pattern is again substantially different from that for other minority groups, although the differences are not as clear when the data are disaggregated by industry as when they are disaggregated by geography. Asian self-employment rates substantially and significantly exceed non-Hispanic white rates in three divisions (TCPU, wholesale trade, and retail trade) and are substantially and significantly below white rates in four other divisions (mining, construction, FIRE, and business services). In the two smallest divisions (entertainment and personal services), differences were neither large nor statistically significant. In two other divisions (manufacturing and professional services), differences were statistically significant but were in excess of the 80 percent substantiality threshold.

Earnings of the self-employed. Like self-employment rates, the economy-wide pattern of disparities in self-employment earnings for blacks, Hispanics, and Native Americans also persists when the PUMS data are disaggregated to the industry division level.

Black self-employment earnings are less than 80 percent of white self-employment earnings in ten of eleven industry divisions. Earnings ratios are lowest in mining (0.49), manufacturing (0.56), and wholesale trade (0.66), and highest in retail trade (0.77), personal services (0.73),

Table 2.20. Estimated average annual earnings of the self-employed and of wage and salary workers, by industry division, and by race and Hispanic origin, 1990

Geographic Division	Race/Ethnic Group	Self-Employment Earnings ($)	Confidence Interval (Lower 95%)	Confidence Interval (Upper 95%)	Wage and salary Worker Earnings
Mining					
	NH White	$50,625	$47,129	$54,121	$42,090
	Black	24,736	13,274	36,197	28,342
	Hispanic	29,097	16,834	41,360	28,535
	Asian	36,980	24,740	49,219	46,962
	Native	53,006	7,630	98,382	32,426
Construction					
	NH White	37,193	36,791	37,596	32,825
	Black	26,608	24,765	28,452	22,401
	Hispanic	28,011	26,592	29,429	22,883
	Asian	38,544	34,598	42,489	36,764
	Native	30,140	25,090	35,190	26,035
Manufacturing					
	NH White	48,112	47,284	48,940	38,009
	Black	27,074	24,010	30,138	27,431
	Hispanic	31,398	28,872	33,924	23,722
	Asian	42,825	38,872	46,779	34,957
	Native	31,232	22,488	39,976	28,300
Transp., Comm. & Public Utils.					
	NH White	41,579	40,619	42,540	37,922
	Black	28,680	26,535	30,825	28,742
	Hispanic	31,679	29,413	33,945	28,766
	Asian	30,815	27,171	34,459	36,437
	Native	34,197	23,897	44,497	30,381
Wholesale Trade					
	NH White	52,838	51,842	53,834	38,440
	Black	34,679	28,456	40,901	24,951
	Hispanic	34,095	31,167	37,023	24,119
	Asian	46,796	42,187	51,406	38,294
	Native	25,504	15,244	35,764	27,606
Retail Trade					
	NH White	38,115	37,642	38,587	30,472
	Black	29,381	26,269	32,494	20,805

Geographic Division	Race/Ethnic Group	Self-Employment Earnings ($)	Confidence Interval (Lower 95%)	Confidence Interval (Upper 95%)	Wage and salary Worker Earnings
	Hispanic	27,227	25,954	28,500	19,975
	Asian	31,262	30,039	32,485	22,744
	Native	23,940	19,224	28,656	22,490
Finance, Insur. & Real Estate					
	NH White	$61,120	$60,169	$62,071	$51,904
	Black	40,532	35,961	45,102	27,506
	Hispanic	49,190	44,429	53,950	29,885
	Asian	51,014	46,397	55,631	43,515
	Native	47,489	21,767	73,210	34,164
Business Services					
	NH White	35,759	35,219	36,299	34,502
	Black	25,907	23,929	27,885	21,744
	Hispanic	25,875	24,030	27,720	21,111
	Asian	35,572	32,863	38,281	32,437
	Native	29,075	21,871	36,278	23,194
Personal Services					
	NH White	31,628	30,706	32,549	27,598
	Black	23,150	20,893	25,406	17,507
	Hispanic	23,987	21,883	26,092	17,457
	Asian	34,009	30,922	37,095	22,287
	Native	16,990	11,435	22,546	18,228
Entertainment Services					
	NH White	40,289	38,606	41,972	34,880
	Black	34,040	25,192	42,889	22,894
	Hispanic	29,604	23,558	35,651	21,181
	Asian	35,013	26,360	43,667	25,837
	Native	12,959	2,813	23,104	21,473
Professional Services					
	NH White	84,803	84,110	85,496	51,391
	Black	60,941	56,757	65,126	25,152
	Hispanic	74,321	70,403	78,240	30,216
	Asian	101,459	97,670	105,247	45,670
	Native	48,900	38,311	59,489	28,057

Source: Author's calculations from Bureau of the Census (1993).

business services (0.72), construction (0.72), and professional services (0.72). Each of these ten differences is also highly statistically significant.[48]

Hispanic self-employment earnings are less than 80 percent of white self-employment rates in nine of eleven industry divisions. Among these nine divisions, earnings ratios for Hispanics are lowest in mining (0.57), manufacturing (0.65), and wholesale trade (0.65), and highest in personal services (0.76), transportation, communications, and public utilities (0.76), and construction (0.75). Each of these nine differences is also statistically significant. In two of eleven divisions, Hispanic self-employment earnings ratios are greater than 80 percent (as well as statistically significant). These sectors are finance, insurance, and real estate (0.81) and professional services (0.88).

The finding that average Hispanic self-employment earnings are 88 percent of non-Hispanic white earnings in the professional services sector contrasts with the other evidence presented for Hispanics so far. This is significant because average self-employment earnings are substantially higher in professional services than in other industry divisions.[49]

Native American self-employment earnings ratios are statistically significant and less than 80 percent in seven of eleven industry divisions. These ratios are lowest in entertainment (0.32), wholesale trade (0.48), personal services (0.54), professional services (0.58), retail trade (0.63), and manufacturing (0.65). Earnings ratios are highest in finance, insurance, and real estate. In the construction, TCPU, and business services divisions the ratios are statistically significant and only slightly higher than 80 percent.

The Asian pattern is again substantially different from that for other minority groups, although as with the self-employment rates just discussed, the differences are not as well defined as they were in the geographic disaggregations. Asians face substantial and significant disparities in only two industry divisions—mining (0.73) and transportation (0.74). Both these differences are statistically significant. In another four divisions (manufacturing, wholesale, retail trade, and finance), disparities are statistically significant, but the ratios are greater than 80 percent (although less than 100 percent). In four others, no statistically significant differences were found (construction, business services, personal services, and entertainment). In only one division, professional services, are Asian self-employment earnings significantly *and* substantially above non-Hispanic white earnings. The high self-employment earnings in this sector may be driving (at least partially) the Asian advantage in earnings observed in the geographic breakdowns presented above.

In Chapter three I will examine whether the disparities in minority self-employment rates and earnings documented in chapter two tend to persist when important economic and demographic covariates such as education, labor market experience, industry, and occupation.

NOTES

[25] Since *Croson* concerned a challenge to local program while *Fullilove* concerned a challenge to a federal program, the *Croson* ruling did not directly affect the federal government's array of MBE programs. In the summer of 1995, however, a 5-4 Supreme Court majority in *Adarand* extended strict scrutiny to the federal government as well, thus formally overturning the *Fullilove* decision.

[26] Other published sources of data on business enterprise or self-employment, such as Internal Revenue Service (IRS) or Social Security Administration (SSA) data do not permit any identification by race or ethnicity.

[27] The 1997 SMOBE will not be published until at least 2001.

[28] Some unpublished special tabulations of SMOBE data from 1987 and 1992 have been produced that provide greater levels of geographic and industrial detail than indicated in Table 2.1. However, the SMOBE sample was not designed to yield particularly precise estimates at such detailed levels. Consequently, the relative standard errors on these unpublished estimates can be quite large in some cases.

[29] The CPS is actually conducted monthly, but the necessary information on income and earnings is only collected once each year.

[30] *See* Table 1.2 and Table 1.3 above. I say "limited" because there were several non-trivial changes made to the SMOBE survey methods between 1987 and 1992 that have handicapped researchers' ability to make comparisons over time with much confidence.

[31] The CPS might possibly yield reliable results for larger states and perhaps for large metropolitan areas as well. For present purposes, I leave a closer examination of this important data source to a future project.

[32] The Census Bureau also produced a 1 percent PUMS product for 1990.

[33] The complete race codes and tribal codes can be found in Appendix C of the 1990 PUMS technical documentation (Bureau of the Census 1992a). Complete Hispanic origin codes are found in Appendix I. These represent the theoretical limits on the amount of racial and ethnic disaggregation possible with the PUMS. Practical limits, as will become clear in chapter three, will be much higher in most cases in order to have large enough numbers of observations available for analysis. For example, although there are Eskimos in Austin, Texas, there are probably not enough of them to derive any useful statistical conclusions regarding discrimination.

[34] A complete list of industry classifications used in the 1990 PUMS appears in Appendix I of the technical documentation (Bureau of the Census 1992a).

[35] A complete list of occupational classifications used in the 1990 PUMS appears in Appendix I of the technical documentation (Bureau of the Census 1992a).

[36] Rather, a more intermediate form of scrutiny is called for. *See*, for example, *United States v. Commonwealth of Virginia*, 518 U.S. 515 (1996).

[37] However, persons working in farming, forestry, or fishing occupations within non-agricultural industries are not excluded.

[38] The PUMS sample design is discussed in more detail in chapter four of Bureau of the Census (1992a).

[39] See Blaug (1985, 458–465) for a discussion of the differences between the Schumpterian and Knightian views of the role of the entrepreneur in economic theory, and the difficulty of reconciling these theories of entrepreneurship and profit with marginal productivity principles and general equilibrium analysis.

[40] There are, no doubt, other causes for these differences as well. On one hand, the Borjas and Bronars sample was substantially smaller in size and covered fewer metropolitan areas than the one used here. On the other, I have incorporated additional restrictions, such as exclusion of the non-profit sector, that Borjas and Bronars did not.

[41] This measure is related to, but not the same as, the self-employment rate. The former measures the percentage of business owners who are minorities while the latter measures the percentage of minorities who are business owners.

[42] The "p-value" measures the probability of rejecting the null hypothesis that self-employment rates do not vary by race or Hispanic origin when it is actually true. Although Type I error is emphasized more in both the legal and the economics literature, it is important to consider Type II error as well. Type II error measures the probability of accepting the null hypothesis when in fact it is false. The "best" statistical test is generally considered to be that which has the lowest Type II probability (the highest "power") for a given Type I probability (say $p = .05$). For the tests just reported, the probability of Type II error is virtually nil, due both to the large sample size and to the distance of the estimated differences from the null hypothesis value of zero.

[43] Unless indicated otherwise, all p-values reported in the text are based on a two-sided test of statistical significance. In many cases, tests of discriminatory differentials are more appropriately based on a one-sided test of significance. In discrimination cases, the courts have usually required p-values of 0.05 or less to establish statistical significance in the two-sided case. The analogous p-value for the one-sided case is half of the two-sided p-value.

[44] *See* 29 C.F.R. § 1607.4(d).

[45] McCloskey and Ziliak (1996) remark that "In a squib published in the American Economic Review in 1985 one of us claimed that '[r]oughly three-quarters of the contributors to the American Economic Review misuse the test of statistical significance.' The full survey confirms the claim, and in some matters strengthens it. We would not assert that every economist misunderstands statistical significance, only that most do, and these some of the best economic scientists" [citations omitted].

[46] Having established the broad similarities between the overall dataset and the full-time, year-round subset, I will restrict the discussion to the latter in this and subsequent sections.

[47] "Other races" were included in the sample tabulations but are not reported separately in this or subsequent tables in this chapter.

[48] In the Entertainment Services division, black earnings are 85 percent of white earnings, but this difference is not statistically significant.

[49] As will be seen below, however, the self-employed Hispanic earnings gap grows to over 20 percent when the amount of labor supplied to the market (*i.e.* number of hours usually worked per week and number of weeks usually worked per year) is held constant (*see* Table 3.5).

CHAPTER 3

Business Disparities and Discrimination

There is no doubt that part of the group differences reported in chapter two are associated with differences in the distribution of individual characteristics and preferences between non-Hispanic whites and minorities. To take just one example, it is well known that personal earnings tend to increase with age. It is also true that the propensity toward self-employment increases with age. Since most minority populations in the U.S. have a lower median age than the non-Hispanic white population, is it possible that the disparities documented in the last chapter are largely—or even entirely—due to differences in the age distribution of minorities compared to non-minorities? Or due to differences in other factors, say, marital status, that are probably unrelated to discrimination? In other words, can the large racial and ethnic disparities observed in self-employment rates and in the earnings of the self-employed be attributed to discrimination or can they be accounted for by differing individual traits among minority and non-minority business owners and by the ordinary processes of market resource allocation? The *Croson* and *Adarand* decisions have raised questions of this sort—questions thought by many to be long settled with respect to employment discrimination against wage and salary workers—to renewed levels of legal and policy importance. This chapter is an attempt to provide some renewed answers to these questions.

These recent developments in constitutional law have coincided with a renewed interest among labor economists in explaining self-employment behavior, an improved array of econometric tools available for the empirical investigation of discrimination, improved computing resources, and the availability of a large representative cross-sectional microdata sample from the 1990 decennial census.[50] Together, they provide the foundation for an empirical microeconomic analysis of self-employment rates and earnings for various minority groups in a variety of geographic areas, industries, and occupations.

Most minority business enterprise disparity studies have documented large economic differentials between minority-owned, women-owned, and non-minority-owned businesses (Enchautegui, et al. 1996). However, few have included any formal attempts to identify what, if any, portion of these disparities could reasonably be attributed to racial, ethnic, or gender discrimination.[51] As with wage and salary employment, theoretical and empirical economic research on self-employment and entrepreneurship has shown that business enterprise is influenced by a number of different quantifiable forces (Brock and Evans 1986; Borjas and Bronars 1989; Evans and Leighton 1989; Meyer 1990; Aronson 1991; Lunn and Perry 1993; Fairlie 1996; Fairlie and Meyer 1996), certain of which may be uninfluenced by discrimination.

Strictly speaking, since business outcomes have multiple influences, it is difficult to determine that discrimination is an important factor simply by observing *gross* racial and ethnic disparities. By the same token, however, the larger the gross disparity is, the less likely it becomes that non-discriminatory factors can account for the entire difference. No doubt it is this simple observation that provides much of the logic behind the EEOC's four-fifths rule for triggering employment discrimination investigations.

Despite this logic, the use of large gross statistical disparities as *prima facie* evidence of discrimination has been harshly criticized by one observer for not providing what the *Croson* decision termed a "strong basis in evidence for [the] conclusion that remedial action was necessary" (*Croson* at 724). George La Noue, a critic of public sector MBE programs, has called this "the most common disparity study fallacy (La Noue 1994b, 490)." While it is true that many disparity studies have not controlled for such factors, I do not agree with La Noue that it is necessarily their obligation to do so. Although *Croson* provides little clear guidance on this matter, following the pattern established in employment discrimination litigation, I would argue that the government entity seeking to initiate or continue an affirmative action program need do no more through its initial disparity study than to establish a *prima facie* case of disparate impact against those groups it seeks to include. For example, by demonstrating that gross statistical disparities facing a given group of minority business owners were both large and statistically significant. At that point, the burden of proof might reasonably be shifted to the plaintiff, who might then seek to demonstrate that the gross disparities in evidence diminish substantially in size or statistical significance (or both) once other influential factors which are unlikely to be correlated with discriminatory activity have been accounted for.

It is worth noting the deliberate addition of the qualifier "unlikely to be correlated with discrimination" to the preceding sentence. Several plaintiff's experts have proposed, and used, factors such as firm revenues, number of employees, years in business, bonding capacity, and other proxies for business size in attempting to rationalize the evidence of large gross statistical disparities that many state and local governments have collected since the *Croson* decision was handed down. To the extent that discrimination is extant, it is highly likely to inhibit both the formation of minority business enterprises and the profits and growth of those enterprises that are formed. For this reason, it is wrong to include such factors when attempting to explain the large size of gross statistical disparities in business enterprise activity.

Despite the obvious flaws in such an approach, a few misguided commentators (*e.g.* La Noue 1994b, Lunn and Perry 1993) have actually argued that this is precisely what needs to be done to explain these disparities. The justification typically offered by these authors has been that measures of size must be included in accounting for racial and ethnic business disparities because larger businesses are more capable of winning sales than smaller firms and because minority firms are typically smaller than non-minority firms. But this simply begs the question. To say that minority market share is relatively smaller because majority firms are relatively larger is merely a tautology. Unfortunately, several federal judges have been taken in by this endlessly circular approach. As economist David Evans (1998, 11) has recently stressed: "[u]sing revenues as a measure of [minority] availability in contracting is like using pay as a measure of qualifications in an equal-pay case."

Furthermore, controlling for factors relating to current size implicitly assumes that the ability of a business enterprise to supply market demand is fixed. Although the elasticity of supply is bound to differ from industry to industry, it is hard to imagine many industries where it is completely inelastic. For example, in the construction industries, which have been the focus of most minority business disparity studies, supply is very elastic. It is well-known that, in general, firms in the construction industry can readily expand in response to market demand by hiring workers, leasing equipment, and utilizing subcontractors (Bourdon and Levitt 1980; Eccles 1981, Evans 1998).

Regardless of whether it is the plaintiff or the defendant who is obliged to explain the cause of any racial or ethnic disparities, what is the likely outcome for conclusions of discrimination when other influential factors are held constant? This is the question addressed in the present chapter. Chapter two demonstrated that black, Hispanic, and Native American males of prime working age had substantially lower self-employment rates and self-employment earnings in 1989–90 than non-Hispanic whites. With only a few exceptions, this situation prevailed for the nation as a whole, in each of four census regions, in each of nine census divisions, and across a variety of major industry and occupation groups. In this final chapter, I use the PUMS data sample described in chapter two to examine whether these disparities persist when a large number of other economic and demographic factors thought to influence self-employment propensities and earnings are simultaneously taken into account. Using multiple regression techniques, I isolate the quantitative impact of race and ethnicity on self-employment propensities and earnings independent of these other economic and demographic characteristics.

Obviously, not all possible non-discriminatory influences are accounted for in any given data set. The PUMS is no exception. Nevertheless, if racial and ethnic disparities remain statistically significant and substantial after controlling for the many influential factors that are available in the PUMS, the case for the continuing existence of discrimination among self-employed minorities is strengthened considerably. Moreover, besides providing a tutorial for the Supreme Court, observing how these disparities change when particular factors are held constant can highlight areas where minority deficits in productive capabilities are greatest, as well as areas where majority-minority differences in market rewards for similar characteristics are largest. My maintained hypothesis is that discrimination, while certainly not the *only* factor responsible for the disparities observed between minority and non-minority business owners, is nevertheless an important one. I do not expect its importance to necessarily remain constant from place to place or industry to industry. Given the substantial size of the gross disparities documented for blacks, Hispanics, and Native Americans in chapter two, however, neither do I expect to find many situations where it is completely—nor even mostly—absent.

This is a less mundane issue than it may at first appear. Although Congress had already officially acknowledged the existence of racial and ethnic discrimination in the construction industry, the majority of justices in *Croson* appeared to believe that Simpson's Paradox was likely to be at work in the national data and that, once more geographically disaggregated analyses were conducted, different conclusions would likely be reached for a substantial number of cases (*Croson* at 726). As a result, constitutional law now requires that government entities wanting to pursue affirmative action in their contracting activities must establish the presence of discrimination against minority businesses in their own "bailiwick," that is, within their own geographic vicinity and within the industries from which they purchase goods and services. As described above in chapter two, the PUMS is far larger and possesses significantly more geographic, industrial, and occupational detail than any other public data source relevant to the study of minority business enterprise. Consequently, among the available public data sources, the PUMS is relatively well-suited to this sort of investigation.[52]

To keep the remaining analysis and the exposition tractable, I limit the geographic scope to the census division level, the industry scope to the SIC division level (*See* Table 2.4), and the occupational scope to the major group level (*See* Table 2.5). In actual practice, the analyst may be required to utilize even finer groupings.

BUSINESS OWNERSHIP ANALYSIS

Background

A small body of recent economic research, most notably Borjas and Bronars (1989), Meyer (1990), Fairlie (1996), and Fairlie and Meyer (1996), has attempted to further our understanding of the underlying causes of large racial and ethnic differentials in self-employment rates. Discrimination, of course, is not the only factor influencing racial and ethnic inequality in the small business sector. Some of these other factors arise from a consideration of the microeconomic underpinnings of business formation and earnings. Kihlstrom and Laffont (1979) and Lucas (1978), drawing on insights from much earlier work by Knight (1965) were among the first to model self-employment behavior from a microeconomic perspective. Lucas' work emphasized the role of unobserved entrepreneurial ability in each agent's choice to start a business or not, while Kihlstrom and Laffont's work highlighted the classic idea of the entrepreneur as risk-bearer. Under this latter model, the individual compares a higher-risk stream of income in the self-employment sector with a lower-risk stream in the wage and salary sector. In a Kihlstrom and Laffont type model, because the income streams are not known with certainty, the individual's aversion to risk enters into his or her hedonic calculation of potential earnings in each sector. Under equilibrium conditions, those with greater tolerance for risk are less likely to choose wage and salary work unless potential wage earnings are relatively high. Those with lower tolerance for risk may not become self-employed even if potential wage earnings are relatively low.

Evans and Jovanovic (1989), drawing on the substantial policy literature documenting the severe under-capitalization problems of small business owners, proposed that levels of available financial capital also influenced the decision to become self-employed. This "liquidity constraints" approach to modeling the self-employment decision is based on the assumption that asset endowments are positively related to the choice of self-employment.

Neither the Kihlstrom-Laffont model nor the Lucas model has been subjected to much direct empirical examination due to the unavailability of actual data on risk tolerance or innate entrepreneurial ability (Fairlie and Meyer 1996). Various measures of assets, on the other hand, are available in several widely used sources of data. Consequently, the Evans and Jovanovic liquidity constraints approach has been the subject of several attempts at empirical testing. Evans and Leighton (1989), Blanchflower and Oswald (1990), and Holtz-Eakin, Joulfaian, and Rosen (1994) all find empirical support for the proposition. Meyer (1990), on the other hand, concludes that assets are not important in influencing self-employment choices.[53]

Although different factors have been highlighted by different investigators, the basic microeconomic approach to understanding self-employment behavior centers around the individual worker's utility-maximizing choice at a given point in time between wage and salary work, on the one hand, and self-employment, on the other; the distributions of workers and entrepreneurs arise as the aggregate outcome of such choices. Borjas and Bronars (1989), Meyer (1990), Fairlie (1996), and Fairlie and Meyer (1996) have demonstrated that many of the factors thought to influence earnings are also important in understanding racial differentials in self-employment rates.

Thus, in the microeconomic model of self-employment behavior, an individual chooses self-employment if expected utility (expected earnings) from self-employment exceeds expected utility from wage and salary employment, given particular levels of risk tolerance. The earnings stream in turn is a function of differing levels of human capital, financial capital, endowments of entrepreneurial ability, and other pro-ductivity-related characteristics.[54] In practice, simplifying assumptions are employed about the functional form of the worker's utility function so that his or her utility maximization problem is reduced to the income maximization problem of choosing between potential earnings streams in each sector.

Methods

Regression analysis is a statistical technique which has become an inte-gral component of empirical analysis when one is concerned with de-scribing the relationship between an outcome, or "dependent," variable and one or more explanatory, or "independent," variables. Although its use is widespread in many areas of both the natural and social sciences, the application of regression in the context of disparity studies has been quite limited. One reason for this is that the data necessary to apply re-gression techniques adequately have, in most cases, been lacking in one or more important respects.[55] Another reason, alluded to earlier, is that the law is still not clear regarding what circumstances, if any, warrant re-gression analyses; or whether the plaintiff or the defendant bears the bur-den of producing them.[56]

With appropriate data, however, regression analysis can lend insight into some of the key questions surrounding the constitutionality of affir-mative action for minority business enterprises. In particular, regression can help answer the question "are the large disparities between minori-ties and non-minorities in business enterprise activity observed in the de-cennial census due to race and ethnicity or are they due to some other, non-discriminatory, factors?"

In order to distinguish the impact of race and ethnicity on self-em-ployment rates from the impact of other influential variables, nine logit regression analyses were conducted—one for each of the nine census ge-ographic divisions. The choice of a particular regression technique should be determined by the specific characteristics of a given investiga-tion. In the case of PUMS business ownership data, the outcome variable is binary. That is, one is either self-employed (dependent variable = 1) or not (dependent variable = 0). For binary outcome variables, an appropri-ate regression method is the probit or logit model.

However, because the PUMS is derived from a complex sample sur-vey, obtaining correct results requires that the standard techniques for any type of regression analysis be modified to accommodate the presence of probability weights, clustering, and stratification in the data. If probability weights are ignored, point estimates will be incorrect. If clustering is ignored, standard errors will most likely be too small. Estimated standard errors are affected by probability weights and stratification as well. All three of these elements have been accounted for in the analyses presented below.[57]

In most applications, probit and logit yield very similar results and there is no general theoretical rule for choosing between them (Greene 1997, 875–876). I chose to use logit for the present analyses because the estimated coefficients are easily transformed into odds ratios. Odds ratios lend themselves more readily to interpretation than do probit regression coefficients or the untransformed logit regression coefficients. The odds ratio measures the odds (probability) of success for members of one group relative to another group. "Success" in the current context means "becomes self-employed." So for example, if group A is, say, only half as successful in becoming self-employed as group B after controlling for a variety of other influential factors, the odds ratio for group A would take on a value of 0.5. Similarly, if group A were twice as successful as group B, their odds ratio would take on a value of 2.0.[58]

After the logit models were computed, the estimated coefficients on the racial and ethnic indicator variables were examined for statistical and substantive significance. If these coefficients, expressed as odds ratios, are less than one in value, statistically significant, and substantively significant, I take this as evidence of the presence of discrimination.

In addition to interpreting individual regression coefficients, it can also be useful to think about the presence of discrimination in terms of *adjusted* self-employment rates and *adjusted* disparity ratios. Two types of adjusted self-employment rates were calculated for this study. The first adjustment provides an indication of what minority self-employment rates would be if minorities possessed the same economic and demographic characteristics as non-Hispanic whites. This calculation yields an indicator of the expected rate of self-employment for each racial and ethnic group in the absence of differences in individual characteristics between groups. That is,

$$P_j^a = 1 \bigg/ \left[n_a \sum_{i=1}^{n_a} (e^{x_{wi} \hat{b} + \hat{a}_j} \big/ 1 + e^{x_{wi} \hat{b} + \hat{a}_j}) \right] \qquad (1)$$

where P_j^a is the adjusted probability of self-employment for non-Hispanic whites if they faced the market structure encountered by minority group j, x_{wi} is the distribution of explanatory variables from the subset of non-Hispanic whites in the sample, $\hat{a}_j$ is the estimated coefficient on the racial indicator variable for minority group j, $\hat{b}$ is the estimated coefficient vector for the remaining variables in the logit regression, and n_a is the number of observations in the overall sample.[59] If minority characteristics are remunerated by the market in basically the same manner as the characteristics of non-Hispanic whites, then the adjusted self-employment rates produced by equation (1) will become close in value to the observed self-employment rate for non-Hispanic whites. Such a result would suggest that the factors driving the gross disparities in self-employment rates are due primarily to differences in characteristics between minorities and non-minorities rather than to racial and ethnic differences in the way the market values those characteristics. To the extent that discrimination has not affected the endowments or acquisition of particular characteristics by minorities, this would constitute evidence against the discrimination hypothesis. Alternatively, if the adjusted rate produced remains close to the observed minority self-employment rate, this indicates that the disparities observed are due mostly to different market treatment for minorities and non-minorities. This would constitute evidence for the discrimination hypothesis. If the adjusted rate ends up somewhere in between, this would be evidence that differences in individual characteristics and discrimination both play a role in explaining observed disparities.

A second adjustment, similar to the first, was also made in which the estimated coefficient vector for non-Hispanic whites was combined with the mean vector of individual characteristics for each of the four minority groups. This adjustment yields the self-employment rate that would be observed for each minority group if the vector of individual characteristics actually possessed by each group was rewarded in the market in a manner equivalent to that for non-Hispanic whites. That is,

$$P_j^b = 1 \Big/ \left[n_b \sum_{i=1}^{n_b} (e^{x_{ij}\hat{b}_w} / 1 + e^{x_{ij}\hat{b}_w}) \right] \tag{2}$$

where x_{ij} represents the values of the explanatory variables for individual i in minority group j, $\hat{b}_w$ is the estimated coefficient vector from the logit regression for non-Hispanic whites, and n_b is the number of observations in the non-Hispanic white sub-sample.[60] If non-Hispanic whites and minorities face essentially the same market structure in self-employment, this second adjusted rate will be very close to the observed minority rate.

Again, assuming that the control variables themselves have not been tainted by discrimination, this would be evidence against the discrimination hypothesis. If not, the adjusted rate will be closer to the observed rate for non-Hispanic whites and this would provide evidence for the discrimination hypothesis.

When these adjusted self-employment rates are compared to those actually observed, the result can be interpreted as a "net" or "adjusted" disparity ratio, as discussed in chapter two. If differences between these two rates are statistically significant and substantially less than 1.0 in value, this is evidence of the ongoing negative effects of discrimination that would seem to meet the *Croson* and *Adarand* strict scrutiny standard of proof.

BUSINESS OWNER EARNINGS ANALYSIS: OAXACA'S MEASURE OF PAY DISCRIMINATION

Background

The second business outcome examined in this chapter for evidence of discrimination is the earnings of the self-employed. Taken together, neoclassical theories of human capital investment and wage discrimination imply that racial differentials in the earnings of the self-employed occur because of differences in average productivity and differences in the way the market treats members of a particular group.

Oaxaca (1973) introduced economists to a technique for decomposing the gross (log) wage differential between two groups of people into two components—one driven by average skill or productivity differences between groups and the other driven by differences in wage structures between groups.[61] This method has been utilized to construct quantitative estimates of pay discrimination among wage and salary workers. As I will show, this method is capable of illuminating the situation of the self-employed as well.[62]

Referring, for simplicity, to the disadvantaged group as "blacks" and to the advantaged group as "whites," let $\overline{w}_w$ and $\overline{w}_b$ represent observed average hourly earnings for self-employed whites and self-employed blacks, respectively.[63] The gross, or unadjusted, wage differential (G_{wb}) between self-employed whites and blacks is then defined as:

$$G_{wb} = \overline{w}_w \big/ \overline{w}_b - 1 \,.$$

(3)

It is assumed that in the absence of discrimination, wage differentials would reflect productivity differences only (Q_{wb}):

$$Q_{wb} = \left. \overline{w}_w^o \middle/ \overline{w}_b^o \right. - 1 \tag{4}$$

Here the superscript o denotes the hypothetical average wages that would be observed in the absence of discrimination. The measure of market discrimination (D_{wb}) can then be defined as:

$$D_{wb} = \frac{\left(\overline{w}_w / \overline{w}_b - \overline{w}_w^o / \overline{w}_b^o \right)}{\overline{w}_w^o / \overline{w}_b^o} \tag{5}$$

Thus, D_{wb} represents the proportionate difference between $G_{wb} + 1$ and $Q_{wb} + 1$.

Several simplifying assumptions are made in order to interpret (5) as a measure of discrimination. Labor supply and individual characteristics must be assumed not to change in the absence of discrimination. It must also be assumed that the standard log wage equation would still hold if discrimination were eliminated. I will maintain these assumptions throughout the remainder of the exercise.

Equations (3)–(5) can be rewritten in terms of the natural logarithm of wages as follows:

$$\ln(G_{wb} + 1) = \ln(Q_{wb} + 1) + \ln(D_{wb} + 1). \tag{6}$$

The first term on the right hand side of equation (6) is the part of the gross wage differential that is due to differences in individual attributes and productivity. The second term on the right hand side is the discrimination coefficient. It is the part of the wage differential that is due to different wage structures between groups—manifested empirically as different regression coefficients.

In the original formulation of Oaxaca (1973) and in most subsequent empirical work, any discriminatory residual detected was necessarily attributed in full to either (a) underpayment of minorities or (b) overpayment of whites, but not both. Many theories, however, suggest that labor market discrimination both lowers wages for minority groups via discrimination and increases them for non-minorities via nepotism (Thurow 1969; Goldberg 1982; Neumark 1988; Oaxaca and Ransom 1994). The market discrimination coefficient in equation (5) measures only the *relative* wage effects of labor market discrimination. It is not possible with this formulation to determine how much of a given differential is due to discrimination and how much is due to nepotism. Generalized versions of the Oaxaca method have recently been introduced by Riemers (1984), Neumark (1988), Cotton (1988) and Oaxaca and Ransom (1994) that allow both phenomena to be present simultaneously. Adding one to both sides of equation (5), taking logs, and re-arranging yields:

$$
\begin{aligned}
\ln(D_{wb} + 1) &= \ln(\overline{w}_w/\overline{w}_b) + \ln(\overline{w}_w^o/\overline{w}_b^o) \\
&= \ln(\overline{w}_w/\overline{w}_w^o) - \ln(\overline{w}_b^o/\overline{w}_b) \\
&= \ln(\delta_{wo} + 1) + \ln(\delta_{ob} + 1)
\end{aligned} \tag{7}
$$

where $\delta_{wo} = \overline{w}_w/\overline{w}_w^o - 1$ and $\delta_{ob} = \overline{w}_b/\overline{w}_b^o - 1$. The discrimination coefficient now contains two distinct terms. The first represents the differential between the observed average wage of whites and their expected average wage in the absence of discrimination. The second term represents the differential between the expected average wage of blacks in the absence of discrimination and their observed average wage. Substituting equation (7) into equation (6) yields

$$
\ln(G_{wb} + 1) = \ln(Q_{wb} + 1) + \ln(\delta_{wo} + 1) + \ln(\delta_{ob} + 1) . \tag{8}
$$

Equation (8) is the generalized decomposition of Oaxaca and Ransom (1994). It shows that the gross differential in log wages consists of three parts: a productivity differential due to differences in individual characteristics, a discrimination differential due to overpayment of the advantaged group, and a discrimination differential due to underpayment of the disadvantaged group.

Method

To derive an empirical estimate of equation (8), the correspondence between its terms and those of an ordinary least squares regression must be recognized. Adding one to each side of equation (3) and taking logs yields:

$$
\ln(G_{wb} + 1) = \ln(\overline{w}_w) - \ln(\overline{w}_b) \tag{9}
$$

Since multiple regression surfaces pass through the means of the independent variables, if standard semi-logarithmic wage equations are estimated separately for whites and blacks, it must be true that:

$$\ln(\overline{w}_w) = \overline{\mathbf{X}}'_w \hat{b}_w \tag{10}$$

$$\ln(\overline{w}_b) = \overline{\mathbf{X}}'_b \hat{b}_b \tag{11}$$

where $\overline{X}'_w$ and $\overline{X}'_b$ are vectors of the means of the independent variables for whites and blacks, respectively, and $\hat{b}_w$ and $\hat{b}_b$ are the estimated ordinary least squares (OLS) coefficients.[64] Subtracting equation (11) from equation (10), equation (9) can be rewritten as:

$$\begin{aligned} \ln(G_{wb} + 1) &= \ln(\overline{w}_w) - \ln(\overline{w}_b) \\ &= \overline{\mathbf{X}}'_w \hat{b}_w - \overline{\mathbf{X}}'_b \hat{b}_b \end{aligned} \tag{12}$$

With a little manipulation, equation (12) can be recast in a form analogous to equation (8). Defining $\hat{b}_o$ as the wage structure that would prevail in the absence of discrimination, adding and subtracting $\overline{\mathbf{X}}'_w b_o$ and $\overline{\mathbf{X}}'_b b_o$ from the right hand side of equation (12), and re-arranging terms yields:

$$\ln(G_{wb} + 1) = \left(\overline{\mathbf{X}}_w - \overline{\mathbf{X}}_b \right)' \hat{b}_o + \overline{\mathbf{X}}'_w \left(\hat{b}_w - \hat{b}_o \right) + \overline{\mathbf{X}}'_b \left(\hat{b}_o - \hat{b}_b \right) . \tag{13}$$

Without exception, the early formulations of the Oaxaca decomposition adopted either the white wage structure or the black wage structure as that which would prevail in the absence of discrimination. It can be seen from equation (13) that both of these are actually special cases of the generalized model. If the white wage structure is adopted as the norm, then $\hat{b}_o = \hat{b}_w$, the middle term of the equation drops out, and the entire discriminatory residual is necessarily attributed to underpayment of blacks. Alternately, if the black wage structure is adopted as the norm, then $\hat{b}_o = \hat{b}_b$, the last term drops out and the entire discriminatory residual is necessarily attributed to overpayment of whites. This equation shows, however, that one is not limited to either of these extremes. Other choices for $\hat{b}_o$ will yield both an overpayment and an underpayment component. The measure of discrimination is intrinsically tied to the choice of $\hat{b}_o$, the hypothetical no-discrimination wage structure.

As Neumark (1988) and Oaxaca and Ransom (1994) point out, the choice of $\hat{b}_o$ is essentially an arbitrary one. In an attempt to make it less so, Neumark extended an extremely simple version of the standard neoclassical discrimination model in order to develop a better rationale for the choice of $\hat{b}_o$. Neumark's model assumes that all firms are identical and competitive. It further assumes that all employers discriminate, so that wage differentials persist in the long run. The firm is assumed to use many different kinds of labor inputs, and to maximize a strictly concave utility function of the form:

$$U = R(\pi, B_1, W_1, \cdots, B_n, W_n) \qquad (14)$$

Output prices are normalized to one. Thus, the profit function is defined as:

$$\pi = f(B_1, W_1, \cdots, B_n, W_n) - \sum_{j=1}^{n} w_{wj} W_j - \sum_{i=1}^{n} w_{bj} B_j \qquad (15)$$

where j indexes different types of jobs. Different types of labor may have different productivities, but *within* each type of labor white and black inputs are assumed homogeneous. Consequently, discrimination "arises" because employers' utility depends both on profits and on the racial composition of each type of labor.[65] Due to status considerations, for example, employers may believe that some types of jobs, say white-collar jobs, are more appropriate for whites and/or less appropriate for blacks than, say, blue-collar jobs (Thurow 1969; Marshall 1974).

Assuming that labor supplies are fixed and that firms are at interior solutions, the first order conditions for utility-maximization are:

$$\left(\frac{\partial U}{\partial \pi}\right)(f_j - w_{wj}) + \left(\frac{\partial U}{\partial W_j}\right) = 0$$

$$\left(\frac{\partial U}{\partial \pi}\right)(f_j - w_{bj}) + \left(\frac{\partial U}{\partial B_j}\right) = 0 \qquad (16)$$

for all $j = [1, \cdots, n]$. Let

$$d_{wj} = \frac{-U_{wj}}{U_\pi}$$

$$d_{bj} = \frac{-U_{bj}}{U_\pi} \qquad (17)$$

These are analogous to Becker-Arrow discrimination coefficients, except that they are not constant. Rather, they vary across each type of labor according to the partial derivative of the utility function with respect to each race-labor type category. Using the equations in (17), the first order conditions in (16) can be rewritten as follows:

$$w_{wj} = f_j - d_{wj}$$
$$w_{bj} = f_j - d_{bj} \tag{18}$$

Since the marginal utility of an additional unit of white (black) labor must be strictly positive (negative) for at least one type of labor, equation (16) implies that

$$w_{wj} \geq f_j \geq w_{bj} \tag{19}$$

which must hold with strict equality at least once.

It is now easy to see how Neumark's model allows for pure discrimination and pure nepotism as special cases, and for some combination of the two otherwise. In the pure discrimination case, the d_w terms are equal to zero. In this case, white wages equal the marginal product of labor type j and black wages are less than this marginal product. In the pure nepotism case, the d_b terms are equal to zero, blacks receive their marginal product, and whites receive more than their marginal product. In the intermediate instance where both d terms are nonzero, whites will receive somewhat more, and blacks somewhat less, than the marginal product of type j labor.

After completing development of his extended model, Neumark (1988, 285–286) comments on how to best represent the wage structure in the absence of discrimination:

> Whether one should accept [$\hat{b}_w$] or [$\hat{b}_b$], or some other set of coefficients as the no-discrimination wage structure, and if so which one, . . . depends on the nature of employers' discriminatory behavior. . . .
> [T]he alternative no-discrimination wage structure derived in this paper is generated by an assumption about employers' discriminatory tastes that imposes neither pure discrimination nor pure nepotism. Instead, it is assumed that employers can be both nepotistic toward [whites] and discriminatory toward [blacks]. This avoids a strong asymmetry in employers' tastes such that, for example, they require higher profits to compensate for hiring [blacks], but are not willing to accept lower profits to hire [whites]. Thus . . . in the absence of discrimination the wages of [whites] would fall, while those of [blacks] would rise.

The cost of relaxing the pure nepotism or pure discrimination assumption is that some other restriction must be imposed on employers' tastes in order to derive an estimable no-discrimination wage structure. The restriction imposed on the utility function is that, within each type of labor, it is homogeneous of degree zero with respect to [white] and [black] labor inputs. . . . Intuitively, this means that employers care only about the relative proportions of [whites] and [blacks], and not absolute numbers. The assumption is less restrictive than it may seem, though, since homogeneity of degree zero must hold only within each type of labor, so that the employer's utility is affected by the distribution of workers, by [race], across types of labor.

Neumark demonstrates that when the utility function is homogeneous of degree zero within each of two types of labor, the no-discrimination (log) wage structure is a weighted average of each group's wage. In the case of many different types of labor, Neumark (1988, 286–289) demonstrates that an OLS criterion can be employed to estimate this wage structure from the pooled white-black regression. That is where **X**,

$$\hat{b}_o = (\mathbf{X'X})^{-1}(\mathbf{X'Y}) = \hat{b} \tag{20}$$

is the matrix of observed independent variables, **Y** is a vector of observed (log) wages, and $\hat{b}$ is the ordinary least squares parameter vector from the pooled regression of whites and blacks. It should be noted that U.S. courts tend to adopt the white wage structure as the no-discrimination wage structure due to a general aversion to lowering white (or male) wages to remedy discrimination against blacks (or females). Nevertheless, for the reasons outlined, the OLS wage structure from the pooled regression may give a better estimate of discrimination under the neoclassical model. In the empirical results presented below for earnings, the nondiscriminatory wage structure is estimated from the pooled regression.

Since I am concerned with self-employment rather than wage and salary employment, it seems natural to ask what relevance an employer discrimination model has to the self-employed. By analogy to the employer discrimination model, it is the *buyers* of the goods and services of the self-employed who are assumed to be the discriminators. Who are these buyers? In some cases they are other businesses who purchase the goods and services of the self-employed as intermediate commodity inputs or labor inputs into their own production processes. This would be the case, for example, for many of the self-employed in the mining, manufacturing, wholesale, and business services industry groups. On the other hand, self-employed business owners in the retail or personal services industry groups are most likely selling their goods and services to final consumers. Self-employed business owners in the remaining industry groups—construction, transportation, and finance—may sell to both types of entities, depending on particular specialties. For example, self-employed construction contractors may sell their services directly to the consumer or indirectly as a subcontractor to another construction firm. In the transportation sector, self-employed truck drivers sell their services to other transportation firms, while self-employed taxicab drivers would generally sell to final consumers.

It is easy to see how the standard employer discrimination model can be recast to apply to self-employed persons selling intermediate goods and services. Conceptually, these individuals can be treated just as any other labor or commodity input into the production process. For self-employed persons selling to final consumers, one can recast the employer's utility maximization problem to a consumer maximization problem. In the latter case, the consumer's (employer's) utility depends not only on the amount of goods and services consumed (profit), but also on the racial and ethnic composition of the sellers of those goods and services. White consumers, for example, may either prefer buying goods and services from white vendors or abhor buying them from black vendors.

Buyer, or consumer, discrimination is not the only source of discrimination facing minority entrepreneurs, however. For example, price discrimination by suppliers of intermediate inputs and by suppliers of financial capital has been documented in a number of disparity studies (*e.g.* Brimmer and Marshall 1990; NERA 1994, Evans 1998). Consequently, discrimination impacts not only the demand for the goods and services of minority entrepreneurs, but their cost schedules as well. Perhaps even more importantly, discrimination also impacts the potential and actual supply of minority entrepreneurs. If feedback effects exist, then potential minority entrepreneurs may be discouraged from going into business for themselves because of anticipated discrimination by buyers, sellers, and lenders. There are many points in the business formation and procurement process where the eventual supply of businesses can be inhibited by discrimination in this way. It is worthwhile to bear in mind that the model used in this study ignores these other sources of discrimination. As such, the analyses presented below allow us only a glimpse into a complex set of interrelationships. An important topic for future research would be to develop data sources that are useful for directly evaluating these other forms of discrimination.

SPECIFICATION OF THE DEPENDENT AND INDEPENDENT VARIABLES

Dependent Variables

The dependent variable for the business ownership exercise is binary. It was created from the PUMS "class of worker" variable, which indicates whether an employed individual owns a business, either incorporated or unincorporated. Persons were classified based on the job in which they reported working the most number of usual hours during the reference year.

The dependent variable in the earnings discrimination exercise is based on each person's 1989 earnings. In the PUMS, it is possible to consider annual earnings, usual weekly earnings, and usual hourly earnings. Since I have not modeled individual labor supply decisions in the present study, I use hourly wages as the dependent variable. Also, I have limited the sample to include only the full-time employed and included average hours worked per week and average weeks worked per year as control variables so as to make this abstraction more tenable.[66]

Independent Variables

Oaxaca decomposition models of the type under discussion here typically assume that the wage structure facing each group can be represented, at its core, by a post-schooling investment model of human capital (Mincer 1970; Johnson 1970). In this formulation both schooling and on-the-job training entail opportunity costs in the form of foregone earnings. The expectation of higher lifetime earnings induces individuals to incur the opportunity costs of human capital investment. Higher lifetime earnings are expected, because individuals with more schooling and on-the-job training are assumed to be more productive.

In empirical applications, the Mincer-Johnson approach generally includes a quadratic term for labor market experience in the wage equation. In many important data sets, including the PUMS, actual labor market experience is not observed. Instead, a proxy variable, based on age and years of schooling, is used.[67] The Mincer-Johnson approach also typically models educational investment as well, either with indicator variables representing different levels of educational attainment or with a linear or quadratic equation in years of schooling. The schooling variables available in the PUMS measure educational attainment more than they do years of schooling and so the indicator variable approach was used here. This human capital investment approach is often supplemented with control variables for other personal and productivity characteristics thought to influence the labor market activity of individuals (*e.g.* Malkiel and Malkiel 1973, 697).

In the present study, the selection of control variables has been guided by several considerations. First, I limited myself to those variables available in the PUMS.[68] Second, since many of the variables found to influence wages and earnings have also been found to influence the self-employment decision, I have tried to include variables that have been found to be important in both types of exercises.[69] Third, to mitigate as far as possible problems of omitted variable bias, I have been fairly liberal in my choices for control variables. This is in keeping with the conservative nature of the *Croson* and *Adarand* decisions, which would not have us attribute to discrimination any portion of a disparity that is more properly attributable to some other, nondiscriminatory, factor. In doing so, however, it is crucial to recognize that to the extent that labor market and business enterprise discrimination generates feedback—a negative effect on the acquisition of relevant attributes such as human capital—the "true" impact of discrimination will be correspondingly understated. If discrimination is still evident under these circumstances, the analysis should be all the more convincing.

The selected explanatory variables fall into five categories: human capital variables (education, experience, health, military service, industry, and occupation), family status variables (marital status, number of workers in the family, number of children, residential mobility), immigration variables (immigrant status, years in U.S. if immigrant, speaks English well), a financial capital variable (interest and dividend income), labor supply (hours worked per week, weeks worked per year), and a set of variables reflecting macroeconomic conditions in local labor markets (*i.e.* unemployment rate, population, population growth between 1980 and 1990, government employment rate, and per capita income). The labor market variables are not included in the PUMS. They were drawn from the Bureau of the Census (1991h) and matched to the PUMS geography using crosswalk tables constructed from data provided in the MABLE/Geocorr database (CIESIN 1996).[70]

RESULTS OF BUSINESS OWNERSHIP ANALYSES

Tables 3.1 and 3.2 present the results of logit regressions for each of the nine census divisions. The tables include the estimated coefficients (expressed as odds ratios), a robust estimate of each coefficient's standard error, the relevant population estimate, the observed self-employment rate, and an adjusted Wald F statistic indicating the joint significance of all coefficients.[71] The Wald F statistic is highly statistically significant in all nine cases, indicating that the regressions have substantial explanatory power—at least when compared to a null, or constant only, model.

Additional measures of goodness-of-fit, such as Pearson or Hosmer-Lemeshow (1989, 136–149) tests have not yet been extended to properly account for complex survey designs. Simple visual inspection can be used to make less formal judgments about fit, however. To do this, the sample for each census division was sorted according to the probability of self-employment predicted by the regression model. Then the sample was divided into ten equal groups, or deciles. In each decile, the observed number of self-employed was then compared to the expected number as predicted by the regression model. In a well-fit model, these two values should be reasonably close to each other within each decile.

For the nine models presented in Tables 3.1 and 3.2, the average difference between observed and expected values within deciles was only 3.6 percent. The median difference was 2.5 percent. In 75 percent of the cases the difference was less than or equal to 5.9 percent and in 99 percent of the cases it was less than or equal to 10.8 percent. Overall, the model fit appears to be quite good.

Control Variables

Education. Turning to the results summarized in Tables 3.1 and 3.2, it is evident that educational attainment has a substantial impact on the likelihood of self-employment. In all nine regressions, the seven indicator variables for educational attainment were jointly statistically significant. As a general rule, additional education appears to substantially improve one's chances of becoming self-employed. The most striking example of this arises in the case of persons with professional degrees, who appear to be three to five times more likely to be self-employed than persons with only a high school diploma.[72] Holders of professional degrees in the Middle Atlantic division, for example, were 2.8 times more likely to be self-employed than corresponding high school graduates, whereas in the East South Central states, such persons were 5.3 times

Table 3.1. Results of logit analyses for the Northeastern and Midwestern census divisions

Variables	New England	Middle Atlantic	East North Central	West North Central
Black	0.5051**	0.5197**	0.5654**	0.5048**
	(0.0531)	(0.0217)	(0.0271)	(0.0574)
Hispanic	0.5433**	0.5881**	0.4851**	0.6949*
	(0.0607)	(0.0240)	(0.0355)	(0.1118)
Asian	0.8682	0.8023**	0.9330	1.0201
	(0.0959)	(0.0376)	(0.0735)	(0.2085)
Native American	0.2847**	0.5846*	0.8048	0.9373
	(0.1143)	(0.1267)	(0.1591)	(0.1786)
Less than High School	0.8809**	0.9075**	1.0063	1.1005~
	(0.0376)	(0.0227)	(0.0288)	(0.0553)
Some College	1.2361**	1.1468**	1.0906**	1.1080**
	(0.0431)	(0.0250)	(0.0253)	(0.0437)
Associate degree	1.0181	1.0307	0.9817	0.9880
	(0.0497)	(0.0323)	(0.0352)	(0.0588)
Bachelor's degree	1.1572**	1.1690**	1.0845**	1.0423
	(0.0455)	(0.0285)	(0.0309)	(0.0498)
Master's degree	0.9476	0.8540**	0.9234~	0.8676~
	(0.0510)	(0.0305)	(0.0399)	(0.0691)
Professional degree	3.0743**	2.8411**	4.0274**	3.2445**
	(0.1999)	(0.1084)	(0.1881)	(0.2639)
Doctorate	1.0350	0.8946~	1.1820~	1.2830~
	(0.1052)	(0.0604)	(0.1049)	(0.1932)
Experience	1.1161**	1.1044**	1.1051**	1.1107**
	(0.0061)	(0.0036)	(0.0042)	(0.0073)
Experience^2	0.9985**	0.9987**	0.9987**	0.9987**
	(0.0001)	(0.0001)	(0.0001)	(0.0001)
Married, spouse present	1.2467**	1.1549**	1.1556**	1.1658**
	(0.0413)	(0.0235)	(0.0278)	(0.0509)
Non-mover	1.2485**	1.1789**	1.2363**	1.2779**
	(0.0318)	(0.0188)	(0.0221)	(0.0391)
Workers in family	0.9088**	0.9302**	0.9557**	0.9692
	(0.0160)	(0.0098)	(0.0118)	(0.0218)
Number of children	1.0305**	1.0411**	1.0349**	1.0387**
	(0.0118)	(0.0072)	(0.0077)	(0.0136)
Immigrant	0.5727**	0.9990	0.7728*	0.7957
	(0.0705)	(0.0583)	(0.0842)	(0.2255)
Years in U.S. (if immigrant)	1.0543**	1.0374**	1.0644**	1.0071
	(0.0135)	(0.0065)	(0.0121)	(0.0312)

Table 3.1. Results of logit analyses for the Northeastern and Midwestern census divisions (*cont.*)

Variables	New England	Middle Atlantic	East North Central	West North Central
Years in U.S.^{2}	0.9990**	0.9991**	0.9986**	1.0002
	(0.0003)	(0.0002)	(0.0003)	(0.0008)
Speaks English well	1.3134*	1.1523**	1.1114	1.1485
	(0.1604)	(0.0599)	(0.1095)	(0.3056)
Health limits work	0.9484	1.0805~	1.1224**	1.2212**
	(0.0593)	(0.0432)	(0.0454)	(0.0799)
Veteran	0.9200*	0.9326*	0.8829**	0.9292
	(0.0370)	(0.0274)	(0.0261)	(0.0428)
Years of military service	0.9507**	0.9459**	0.9651**	0.9525**
	(0.0081)	(0.0075)	(0.0070)	(0.0097)
Interest & dividend income	1.2325**	1.2467**	1.2807**	1.2483**
	(0.0189)	(0.0122)	(0.0158)	(0.0290)
Usual weeks worked per year	0.9511**	0.9575**	0.9650**	0.9703**
	(0.0040)	(0.0025)	(0.0030)	(0.0051)
Usual hours worked per week	1.0515**	1.0528**	1.0496**	1.0497**
	(0.0014)	(0.0008)	(0.0009)	(0.0015)
Industry Indicator Variables				
Mining	2.4205**	1.1545	1.6154**	1.2394
	(0.6537)	(0.1698)	(0.2400)	(0.2405)
Construction	7.8550**	5.6659**	8.2428**	7.1051**
	(0.3813)	(0.1756)	(0.2814)	(0.4447)
Transp., comm, pub. utils.	1.8869**	2.0952**	2.6688**	2.1316**
	(0.1184)	(0.0696)	(0.1004)	(0.1370)
Wholesale trade	2.0923**	2.1683**	2.5575**	2.0008**
	(0.1239)	(0.0760)	(0.0989)	(0.1355)
Retail trade	4.3173**	3.6839**	4.4914**	3.2701**
	(0.1985)	(0.1077)	(0.1480)	(0.1963)
Finance, insur, real estate	3.1783**	2.0086**	4.5602**	4.6121**
	(0.1679)	(0.0698)	(0.1718)	(0.3044)
Business and repair services	10.1535**	7.7454**	11.2070**	11.9392**
	(0.4981)	(0.2457)	(0.3930)	(0.7372)
Personal services	11.9597**	9.6655**	16.2316**	12.9588**
	(0.9374)	(0.4638)	(0.9085)	(1.2536)
Entertainment and recreation	7.8732**	5.9424**	8.8594**	7.1209**
	(0.9550)	(0.3762)	(0.6902)	(0.9854)
Professional services	7.8169**	6.6935**	9.1754**	9.0833**
	(0.3736)	(0.2061)	(0.3286)	(0.5949)

Occupation Indicator Variables				
Exec., admin., and managerial	1.7853** (0.1364)	2.0892** (0.0995)	2.9917** (0.1559)	2.3158** (0.2066)
Professional specialty	1.7467** (0.1397)	2.1431** (0.1072)	2.3309** (0.1315)	2.0418** (0.1978)
Technicians & related support	0.6108** (0.0664)	0.6241** (0.0440)	0.8639~ (0.0679)	0.5926** (0.0858)
Sales	2.4641** (0.1916)	3.0752** (0.1479)	4.2171** (0.2217)	3.2831** (0.2950)
Administrative support	0.6729** (0.0676)	0.5853** (0.0380)	0.7455** (0.0550)	0.6207** (0.0799)
Protective service	0.2650** (0.0646)	0.0351** (0.0359)	0.4707 (0.3737)	0.3724** (0.1172)
Other service	1.2707** (0.1116)	0.2366** (0.0357)	0.3339** (0.0672)	1.3893** (0.1452)
Farming, forestry, and fishing	5.4460** (1.0916)	0.9653 (0.0525)	1.6840** (0.1024)	3.9240** (1.0050)
Construction trades	3.0783** (0.2402)	2.3048** (0.3468)	3.4591** (0.5346)	3.2204** (0.3002)
Precision production and craft	1.3138** (0.0997)	2.9089** (0.1432)	3.5459** (0.1893)	1.4288** (0.1252)
Transport. & material moving	0.6898** (0.0597)	1.4532** (0.0686)	1.5832** (0.0807)	1.0441 (0.0959)
Local Labor Market Variables				
Unemployment rate	1.0357 (0.0311)	1.0937~ (0.0541)	1.1328* (0.0615)	1.0216 (0.0226)
Population	1.0000** (0.0000)	1.0880** (0.0158)	0.9988 (0.0094)	1.0000** (0.0000)
Population growth	1.0043 (0.0027)	1.0000 (0.0000)	1.0000** (0.0000)	1.0125** (0.0024)
Government employment rate	1.0000 (0.0001)	1.0043* (0.0021)	1.0056** (0.0021)	1.0001* (0.0001)
Per capita income	1.0000** (0.0000)	1.0002** (0.0000)	1.0001 (0.0000)	0.9999** (0.0000)
Adjusted Wald $F(k,d)$	191.22 (53, 88701)	464.4 (54, 242864)	434.64 (54, 239996)	138.26 (53, 74696)
Population estimate	1,895,227	5,177,291	5,377240	1,798,950
Self-employment rate	0.1430	0.1421	0.1083	0.1264

Source: Author's calculations using Bureau of Census (1993).

Note: (1) Standard errors in parentheses with p<0.10 = ~, p<0.05 = *, p<0.01 = **; (2) The adjusted Wald F statistic is a survey-based test of the joint statistical significance of all regressors. k is the numerator degrees of freedom and is equal to the number of regressors in the model. d is the denominator degrees of freedom and is equal to the number of samples primary sampling units (PSUs) minus the number of strata.

Table 3.2. Results of logit analyses for the Southern and Western census divisions

Variables	South Atlantic	East South Central	West South Central	Mountain	Pacific
Black	0.5392**	0.4919**	0.5025**	0.4941**	0.6366**
	(0.0159)	(0.0351)	(0.0246)	(0.0697)	(0.0296)
Hispanic	0.8202**	1.2429	0.6371**	0.6131**	0.5262**
	(0.0341)	(0.2537)	(0.0248)	(0.0386)	(0.0153)
Asian	1.0471	1.3480	1.0587	1.1417	0.8414**
	(0.0642)	(0.3226)	(0.0847)	(0.1384)	(0.0231)
Native American	1.0268	1.0985	0.9221	0.6298*	0.7659**
	(0.1339)	(0.3525)	(0.0900)	(0.1205)	(0.0733)
Less than High School	0.9224**	1.0324	0.9486	0.8817*	0.8943**
	(0.0207)	(0.0473)	(0.0305)	(0.0493)	(0.0242)
Some College	1.1927**	1.1702**	1.2274**	1.2596**	1.1796**
	(0.0245)	(0.0503)	(0.0334)	(0.0504)	(0.0244)
Associate degree	1.1019**	0.9619	1.1098*	0.9984	1.0590*
	(0.0341)	(0.0723)	(0.0509)	(0.0617)	(0.0298)
Bachelor's degree	1.2208**	1.2223**	1.3143**	1.2968**	1.1967**
	(0.0293)	(0.0628)	(0.0423)	(0.0624)	(0.0287)
Master's degree	1.0766*	1.0865	1.2050**	1.1026	1.0603~
	(0.0390)	(0.0930)	(0.0593)	(0.0777)	(0.0348)
Professional degree	3.6816**	5.3225**	4.7753**	4.0306**	3.2009**
	(0.1434)	(0.4686)	(0.2554)	(0.3197)	(0.1198)
Doctorate	1.3121**	1.5341**	1.5693**	1.8728**	1.2779**
	(0.0886)	(0.2422)	(0.1467)	(0.2239)	(0.0741)
Experience	1.1054**	1.1150**	1.1009**	1.1176**	1.1132**
	(0.0035)	(0.0078)	(0.0048)	(0.0075)	(0.0036)
Experience^2	0.9987**	0.9986**	0.9989**	0.9986**	0.9987**
	(0.0001)	(0.0001)	(0.0001)	(0.0001)	(0.0001)
Married, spouse pres.	1.2737**	1.2152**	1.1833**	1.1297**	1.2202**
	(0.0249)	(0.0541)	(0.0324)	(0.0452)	(0.0223)
Non-mover	1.3363**	1.3275**	1.3892**	1.3528**	1.2250**
	(0.0196)	(0.0423)	(0.0274)	(0.0394)	(0.0176)
Workers in family	0.9584**	0.9834	0.9817	0.9799	0.9286**
	(0.0103)	(0.0229)	(0.0142)	(0.0220)	(0.0098)
Number of children	1.0115~	1.0242~	1.0186*	1.0462**	1.0251**
	(0.0067)	(0.0144)	(0.0085)	(0.0117)	(0.0063)
Immigrant	0.8783*	0.4967*	0.9759	0.6944*	1.0987*
	(0.0574)	(0.1693)	(0.0998)	(0.1289)	(0.0505)
Years in U.S. (if immig.)	1.0561**	1.0767~	1.0208~	1.0425*	1.0360**
	(0.0080)	(0.0424)	(0.0124)	(0.0210)	(0.0056)

Years in U.S.[2]	0.9987**	0.9982~	0.9996	0.9992	0.9989**
	(0.0002)	(0.0011)	(0.0003)	(0.0005)	(0.0001)
Speaks English well	0.9268	0.8549	1.4537**	1.2000	1.1039*
	(0.0498)	(0.2264)	(0.1033)	(0.1843)	(0.0439)
Health limits work	1.0983**	1.1478~	1.2090**	1.0721	1.1063**
	(0.0365)	(0.0825)	(0.0535)	(0.0701)	(0.0383)
Veteran	0.9161**	0.9204~	0.8624**	0.8922**	0.8997**
	(0.0179)	(0.0409)	(0.0231)	(0.0359)	(0.0191)
Years of military service	0.9667**	0.9714**	0.9690**	0.9668**	0.9608**
	(0.0027)	(0.0071)	(0.0038)	(0.0060)	(0.0035)
Interest & div. income	1.2320**	1.3361**	1.2272**	1.2669**	1.1993**
	(0.0125)	(0.0344)	(0.0175)	(0.0279)	(0.0107)
Usual weeks worked	0.9590**	0.9615**	0.9682**	0.9705**	0.9671**
	(0.0025)	(0.0052)	(0.0033)	(0.0049)	(0.0023)
Usual hours worked	1.0434**	1.0415**	1.0268**	1.0327**	1.0423**
	(0.0007)	(0.0015)	(0.0007)	(0.0012)	(0.0007)
Industry Indicator Variables					
Mining	0.7752~	0.8141	1.5171**	0.8015	0.7472*
	(0.1175)	(0.1759)	(0.0928)	(0.1344)	(0.1099)
Construction	5.4707**	7.5169**	5.1287**	4.4142**	5.0714**
	(0.1668)	(0.4699)	(0.2052)	(0.2727)	(0.1502)
Transportation	1.9139**	1.9830**	1.7739**	1.2849**	1.7177**
	(0.0658)	(0.1398)	(0.0795)	(0.0931)	(0.0587)
Wholesale trade	1.9767**	2.2502**	1.9440**	1.6028**	1.8419**
	(0.0703)	(0.1635)	(0.0896)	(0.1147)	(0.0614)
Retail trade	2.8347**	3.7771**	3.1232**	2.4301**	2.9349**
	(0.0863)	(0.2336)	(0.1239)	(0.1474)	(0.0814)
Finance, etc.	3.3899**	3.4710**	3.9107**	3.5057**	3.4826**
	(0.1146)	(0.2602)	(0.1735)	(0.2243)	(0.1047)
Business services	8.2553**	13.1318**	9.2949**	7.5291**	8.1790**
	(0.2577)	(0.8655)	(0.3760)	(0.4542)	(0.2324)
Personal services	5.8293**	10.0927**	8.3627**	3.5261**	7.1361**
	(0.2867)	(1.0203)	(0.5531)	(0.3078)	(0.3206)
Entertainment	5.0640**	8.4744**	7.1726**	3.0279**	4.6272**
	(0.3162)	(1.3327)	(0.6754)	(0.3318)	(0.2335)
Professional services	6.7333**	7.3133**	7.3805**	6.0107**	6.8540**
	(0.2193)	(0.5108)	(0.3133)	(0.3672)	(0.1902)
Occupation Indicator Variables					
Executive & managerial	1.8059**	2.8656**	1.8392**	1.4695**	1.8204**
	(0.0825)	(0.2856)	(0.1044)	(0.1322)	(0.0785)
Professional specialty	1.4985**	2.5117**	1.3995**	1.1347	1.5910**
	(0.0733)	(0.2736)	(0.0859)	(0.1082)	(0.0719)
Technicians	0.5663**	1.0987	0.5578**	0.5049**	0.6033**
	(0.0372)	(0.1568)	(0.0463)	(0.0607)	(0.0361)

Table 3.2. Results of logit analyses for the Southern and Western census divisions (*cont.*)

Variables	South Atlantic	East South Central	West South Central	Mountain	Pacific
Sales	2.5418**	4.1557**	2.5441**	2.0456**	2.5350**
	(0.1173)	(0.4152)	(0.1451)	(0.1864)	(0.1116)
Administrative support	0.5027**	0.8891	0.5165**	0.4212**	0.5465**
	(0.0326)	(0.1236)	(0.0412)	(0.0521)	(0.0321)
Protective service	0.2807**	0.1994**	0.2242**	0.2314**	0.2701**
	(0.0341)	(0.0773)	(0.0419)	(0.0516)	(0.0329)
Other service	1.0190	1.6065**	0.9914	0.8092*	0.9459
	(0.0553)	(0.1913)	(0.0684)	(0.0856)	(0.0479)
Farming	2.5722**	10.5182**	1.6724**	1.0195	1.3017*
	(0.2928)	(2.3045)	(0.2866)	(0.2761)	(0.1657)
Construction trades	2.6058**	3.8353**	2.6378**	1.6508**	2.0355**
	(0.1204)	(0.3832)	(0.1524)	(0.1549)	(0.0945)
Precision production	1.2960**	1.7935**	1.2997**	1.0207	1.2369**
	(0.0581)	(0.1739)	(0.0718)	(0.0926)	(0.0538)
Transportation	0.8944*	1.0932	0.8933~	0.5869**	0.7099**
	(0.0431)	(0.1123)	(0.0536)	(0.0590)	(0.0341)
Local Labor Market Variables					
Unemployment rate	1.0199**	0.9647*	0.9318**	1.0067	0.9839**
	(0.0067)	(0.0145)	(0.0093)	(0.0210)	(0.0058)
Population	1.0000**	1.0000**	1.0000	1.0000**	1.0000
	(0.0000)	(0.0000)	(0.0000)	(0.0000)	(0.0000)
Population growth	1.0047**	1.0038	1.0099**	0.9947**	1.0073**
	(0.0005)	(0.0031)	(0.0011)	(0.0011)	(0.0010)
Gov't. employment rate	1.0001*	1.0001	0.9999~	1.0006**	1.0000
	(0.0000)	(0.0001)	(0.0001)	(0.0001)	(0.0000)
Per capita income	1.0000**	0.9999**	0.9999**	1.0000**	1.0000**
	(0.0000)	(0.0000)	(0.0000)	(0.0000)	(0.0000)
Adjusted Wald $F(k,d)$	470.39	124.32	770.84	117.65	500.51
	(53, 237823)	(53, 62897)	(53, 141567)	(53, 59169)	(53, 232210)
Population estimate	5,112,484	1,382,730	3,068,829	1,346,845	5,218,265
Self-employment rate	0.1426	0.1284	0.1401	0.1420	0.1522

Source: Author's calculations using Bureau of Census (1993).
Note: (1) Standard errors in parentheses with $p<0.10 = \sim$, $p<0.05 = *$, $p<0.01 = **$; (2) The adjusted Wald F statistic is a survey-based test of the joint statistical significance of all regressors. k is the numerator degrees of freedom and is equal to the number of regressors in the model. d is the denominator degrees of freedom and is equal to the number of samples primary sampling units (PSUs) minus the number of strata.

more likely to be self-employed. The coefficients on the professional degree indicator variable are highly statistically significant in all nine divisions.

Possessing a bachelor's degree or a doctoral degree also appears to substantially improve one's chances of becoming self-employed relative to high school graduates, although not as much as in the case of professional degrees. Odds ratios on the bachelor's degree indicator variable range from a low of 1.04 in the West North Central to a high of 1.31 in the West South Central. Coefficients on the bachelor's degree indicator variable are highly statistically significant in all but the West North Central division. In seven of the nine divisions, holding a doctoral degree has a large positive impact on the probability of being self-employed relative to high school graduates. In the East North Central, Ph.D's are 18 percent more likely to be self-employed than high school graduates. In the Mountain division, the figure is 87 percent. All seven of these odds ratios are statistically significant. In New England, these is no evidence that holding a doctoral degree improves the probability of self-employment. The coefficient on the doctoral indicator variable in the regression for New England is 1.04, but is not statistically significantly different from one. Only in the Middle Atlantic division does it seem that holding a doctoral degree decreases the likelihood of self-employment relative to those with a high school diploma. Here the estimated odds ratio is 0.89 and is statistically significant.

It also appears that persons who have attended some college, but who do not possess a degree of any kind, have a substantially higher likelihood of being self-employed than those with only a high school education. The improvement ranges from a low of 9 percent in the East North Central to a high of 26 percent in the Mountain states. These differences are highly statistically significant in all nine divisions. Possession of an Associate Degree increases the relative likelihood of self-employment in three divisions but appears to have no statistically significant affect in six others.

The master's degree is the only educational attainment category that isn't strongly associated with increases in the probability of self-employment. In five of the nine divisions, holders of such degrees actually had lower probabilities of self-employment than high school graduates. In only one division, the West South Central, did holding a master's degree substantially improve increase the probability of self-employment.

Labor market experience. The logit results show that self-employment probabilities also rise with potential labor market experience, but at a decreasing rate. The sizes of the estimated experience coefficients are very similar, and both elements of the quadratic specification of experience are highly statistically significant in all nine divisions. According to the fitted model, additional labor market experience ceases to improve the probability of self-employment, on average, between one's 30s and early 40s. This finding is consistent with previous cross-sectional studies of self-employment (Aronson 1991, 22–23).

Family status. Turning next to the family status variables included in each regression, it is evident that these factors too exert quite a strong influence on the probability of being self-employed. The four different family status variables (married, number of children, number of workers in family, and lived in same residence past five years) were jointly statistically significant in all nine regressions.

Considering briefly the individually estimated coefficients on the family status variables, the reader can see that being married, with spouse present, strongly increases the probability of self-employment in all nine divisions. This increase in probability ranges from a low of 13 percent in the Mountain states to a high of 27 percent in the South Atlantic. All these odds ratios are highly statistically significant.

Larger families also appear to be associated with higher self-employment probabilities. Each additional child raises the odds of self-employment between about 2 percent and 5 percent, depending on geographic location. The coefficient on the variable measuring number of children in the household is positive and statistically significant in all nine divisions.

In contrast, as more members of the household join the labor force, other things equal, the probability of self-employment falls. The odds ratio associated with number of workers in the family ranges between approximately 0.91 and 0.98 depending on division. This reduction is statistically significant in five of the nine divisions.

Of all the family status variables controlled for in these nine regressions, residing in the same house during the five years prior to the census was the factor most strongly associated with an increased probability of being self-employed. The estimated odds ratio on this variable is highly statistically significant in all nine census divisions and ranges from a low of 1.18 in the Middle Atlantic to 1.39 in the West South Central states.

Immigrant status. A substantial body of literature documents the self-employment propensities of immigrants (e.g., Borjas 1986). The nine logit regressions in Tables 3.1 and 3.2 include an indicator variable for whether or not a given individual is an immigrant and, if so, the number of years spent in the U.S. Also included in the specification is the square of the number of years spent in the U.S. and an indicator variable for whether a person speaks English well. The coefficients on these four variables are jointly significant in all but the West North Central and the East South Central divisions.

The odds ratios on immigrant status are substantially less than one in eight of the nine census divisions, although these coefficients are statistically significant in only five of these divisions. The odds ratio on immigrant status in the Pacific division, in contrast to the other eight divisions, is positive and statistically significant, indicating that immigrants are about 10 percent more likely to be self-employed than non-immigrants in the Pacific states.

The two variables measuring the years immigrants have spent in the U.S., indicate that self-employment propensities for immigrants tend to increase over time, albeit at a decreasing rate. The positive effect of longevity in the U.S. on immigrant self-employment propensities, other things equal, peaks at about 17 years in the Pacific division versus 27 years in New England. In the remaining divisions the peak occurs between 21 years and 25 years after immigration.

The coefficient on the dummy variable indicating that an individual speaks English well is greater than one and statistically significant in seven of nine divisions, indicating that facility with English enhances one's likelihood of owning a business relative to persons who have a problem speaking English. In the other two divisions, the odds ratio is less than one, but is not statistically significant.

Disability. Persons with a work-limiting disability are substantially more likely to become self-employed in eight of the nine divisions studied. The increase runs between about 10 percent in the South Atlantic states to about 22 percent in the West North Central states. In seven of these eight divisions, the odds ratio is statistically significant. In New England the odds ratio is less than one (0.95), but is not statistically significant.

Military service. Being a veteran of the military appears to reduce one's odds of self-employment relative to non-veterans by between 8 percent and 14 percent, depending on geographic location. This result,

which is statistically significant in all nine divisions, contrasts with results from earlier studies based on 1980 census data (*e.g.* Borjas and
Bronars 1989) that found veteran status to increase the likelihood of self-
employment. Possibly, this reflects different self-employment patterns between Vietnam-era veterans, on the one hand, and Korean Conflict and
World War II veterans, on the other, since there has been substantial sample
attrition of the latter since the 1980 census. It may also reflect the influence
of the included control variable for years of military service. This variable,
although highly statistically significant in the regressions performed here,
has been absent in earlier empirical studies of self-employment.

Assets. Interest and dividend income, the proxy variable for financial capital, has a large and statistically significant influence on self-employment propensities in all nine divisions. Other things equal, each
additional ten thousand dollars of interest and dividend income increases
the likelihood of self-employment between 20 percent and 34 percent,
depending on geographic division. This is consistent with the findings of
Evans and Jovanovic (1989) and others concerning the liquidity constraints facing business owners.

Labor supply. The variables tracking labor supply also appear to
have substantial explanatory power. In all nine divisions, the self-employed work noticeably fewer weeks per year but noticeably more hours
per week. The odds ratio for usual weeks worked per year ranges between 0.95 and 0.97, indicating that each additional week usually
worked in a year is associated with between a 3 percent and a 5 percent
reduction in the probability of self-employment. The odds ratio for usual
hours worked per week ranges between 1.03 and 1.05. Coefficients on
both of these variables are highly statistically significant in all nine geographic divisions. Moreover, the two variables are jointly statistically
significant in all nine regressions.

Industry. The industry indicator variables are highly statistically
significant and also display a consistent pattern across divisions. Odds
ratios are larger than one in almost every case, reflecting the very low
level of self-employment in the manufacturing sector (which is the reference group). Further, the relative position of industry divisions in terms
of the estimated odds ratio is fairly constant both across and within geographic divisions. Industry sectors with the largest self-employment
probabilities include all the service sectors and the construction sector.

Self-employment propensities in the finance, retail trade, and wholesale trade sectors are somewhat lower, but still are two to four times greater than in the manufacturing sector. The ten industry indicator variables are jointly statistically significant in all nine regressions. Moreover, the individually estimated coefficients are highly statistically significant in almost every instance.

Occupation. Like the industry indicator variables, the eleven occupational indicator variables are jointly significant in all nine regressions and the individual coefficients are statistically significant in most cases. The reference group for the occupational indicator variables is the "Operators, Fabricators, and Laborers" group. Groups such as protective services, administrative support, and technical support tend to have lower self-employment probabilities than in the operator group, while most other occupational groups included tend to have higher probabilities. The highest self-employment propensities are observed in the sales occupations and the construction trades, followed by executive, administrative, and managerial occupations and professional specialty occupations.

Local macroeconomic conditions. The variables controlling for local labor markets were jointly statistically significant in all nine regressions. Individual coefficients were also statistically significant in about 70 percent of the cases. The odds ratios for population size, population growth, and the government employment rate are greater than one in almost every instance. The odds ratios associated with local unemployment rates and local per capita income levels are more mixed.

Race and Ethnicity

As the *Croson* decision alluded, and as the preceding pages demonstrate, there are a number of factors other than race or ethnicity that appear to exert strong influences on the likelihood of being self-employed. Educational attainment, labor market experience, family structure, immigration status, disability, military service, assets, labor supply choices, industry, and occupation all appear to play a role. Given the strength of some of these influences, and the likelihood that they are distributed somewhat differently between minority and non-minority populations, what has become of the racial and ethnic disparities documented in chapter two?

Incredibly, even after holding all these other factors constant, Tables 3.1 and 3.2 show that the probability of self-employment for blacks is still only about half that of non-Hispanic whites. The estimated odds ratio for blacks, which can be interpreted as a disparity ratio, ranges from a low of 0.49 in the East South Central states to a high of 0.64 in the Pacific states. This result is highly statistically significant in all nine regressions.

Similarly for Hispanics, in seven of nine geographic divisions the probability of self-employment is only about half to two-thirds of the corresponding probability for non-Hispanic whites. These differences are all highly statistically significant. In the East South Central division, however, there is no statistically significant difference between Hispanic self-employment probabilities and non-Hispanic white probabilities. In the South Atlantic division, the Hispanic disparity ratio is 0.82 (and statistically significant), slightly above the 80 percent substantiality threshold discussed in chapter two.

Native American disparity ratios are large and statistically significant in four divisions—New England, Middle Atlantic, Mountain, and Pacific. In three other divisions—East North Central, West North Central, and West South Central—disparity ratios are less than one but greater than the 80 percent substantiality threshold. These disparity ratios are not statistically significantly different from one, however. In the two remaining divisions, disparity ratios are slightly higher than one and are not statistically significant. This lack of statistical significance may stem from the relatively small numbers of self-employed Native Americans captured in the PUMS sample coupled with the relatively large number of regressors in the model.

Asian disparity ratios are less than one and statistically significant in the Middle Atlantic and Pacific divisions. In the Middle Atlantic the estimated odds ratio is 0.80 and in the Pacific it is 0.84. In New England and the East North Central, the odds ratio for Asians is less than one but is not statistically significant. In the remaining five divisions the estimated odds ratios are greater than one but are not statistically significant.

In summary, these nine logit regressions have produced strong evidence of racial and ethnic discrimination inhibiting black and Hispanic business formation, even when business owners are *similarly situated*. There is evidence of discrimination against Native American entrepreneurs as well, but the ability to draw inferences for this latter group is hampered in several instances by small sample size coupled with the unbalanced nature of the dependent variable. In contrast, there is little evidence of disparities facing Asians once education, experience and other factors have been accounted for.

Adjusted Self-Employment Rates

As mentioned earlier, I have calculated two other statistics designed to highlight the effect of race and ethnicity on the propensity to start a business enterprise—independent of other influential factors. The first measure takes the distribution of independent variables possessed by non-Hispanic whites and evaluates it according to the market structure facing each minority group, as represented by the estimated coefficient vector for each minority group. This adjustment provides an indication of what minority self-employment rates would look like if minorities possessed the same characteristics as non-Hispanic whites.[73]

As described above in the case of earnings differences, the difference between the observed non-minority self-employment rate and the observed minority self-employment rate can be thought of, in the simplest case, as consisting of two components. One part of the difference can be attributed to differences in the distribution of individual characteristics between the two groups while the second portion of the difference can be attributed to discrimination. That is, the difference in self-employment rates that is accounted for by racial and ethnic differences in the way the market evaluates a given set of individual characteristics.

It is readily shown that the difference in self-employment rates attributable to differences in individual characteristics between groups is equal to the difference between the adjusted self-employment rate described above and the observed minority self-employment rate. The portion attributable to discrimination is represented by the difference between the non-Hispanic white self-employment rate and this adjusted self-employment rate.[74]

For example, Table 3.3 shows that the observed self-employment rate for non-Hispanic whites in New England is 15.0 percent, while the observed rate for blacks is 5.4 percent—a difference of 9.6 percentage points (column A). If blacks possessed the non-Hispanic white distribution of individual characteristics but faced their own estimated market structure, the model predicts a black self-employment rate of 9.1 percent (column B). Of the overall difference in self-employment rates of 9.6 percentage points, 3.7 percentage points (9.1 − 5.4) are due to differences in individual characteristics. This amounts to 38.5 percent of the total difference. The remaining 5.9 percentage points (15.0 − 9.1), amounting to 61.5 percent of the total difference, reflect discrimination.

Not only is the adjusted rate useful in determining what portion of a racial or ethnic self-employment rate differential is related to discrimination, it can also be used to form a "net" or "adjusted" disparity ratio in the sense used at the beginning of this chapter. Continuing with New England as an example, the figure in column B for blacks suggests that even if there were no differences in individual attributes between whites and blacks, the black self-employment rate would be only 9.1 percent. Compared to the observed self-employment rate for whites of 15.0, this yields an adjusted disparity ratio with a value of 0.61 (9.1 ÷ 15.0), far below the 80 percent substantiality threshold and statistically significant as well.[75]

The second adjusted measure calculates the self-employment rate for each minority group that would be obtained if the individual characteristics possessed by each minority group were remunerated according to the market structure facing non-Hispanic whites, as represented by the estimated coefficient vector for non-Hispanic whites.[76] Like the first adjustment, it can also be used to allocate the difference in self-employment rates between discriminatory and non-discriminatory components as well as to construct an adjusted disparity ratio.[77]

For example, in Table 3.3, the self-employment rate for blacks is predicted to be 9.5 percent if blacks faced the same estimated market structure as non-Hispanic whites (column C). The overall difference in self-employment rates of 9.6 percentage points can be divided into a 5.5 percentage point difference (15.0 – 9.5) in individual attributes and a 4.1 percentage point difference (9.5 – 5.4) attributable to discrimination. Using this measure, almost 43 percent of the difference in self-employment rates between whites and blacks is attributable to discrimination (column E).[78] An adjusted disparity ratio can also be constructed. In this case, the ratio is formed by comparing the observed self-employment rate for blacks (5.4 percent) to the self-employment rate blacks are predicted to have (9.5 percent) if their own attributes were compensated in a manner comparable to non-Hispanic whites. Dividing the latter figure into the former yields a disparity ratio of 0.57 (5.4 ÷ 9.5) (column D).

To recap, column A of Table 3.3 contains the observed self-employment rates in each division for each minority group.[79] Column B contains the self-employment rate predicted by the model if each minority group possessed the same distribution of independent variables as non-Hispanic whites. Column C contains the self-employment rate that would be expected if each minority group faced the market structure that obtains for non-Hispanic whites. Column D provides an adjusted disparity ratio, defined as the observed minority self-employment rate from column A divided by the adjusted self-employment rate in column C.[80] Column E indicates the portion of the difference in self-employment rates that is attributable to discrimination as opposed to differences in individual economic and demographic characteristics.

A comparison of column C and column A shows that if minority entrepreneurs faced the same market structure as non-Hispanic whites, their self-employment rates would be much closer in value to those of non-Hispanic whites. The black self-employment rate in New England, for example, would be 9.5 percent compared to the observed rate of 5.4 percent. This yields an adjusted disparity ratio of 0.57—far below the 80 percent substantiality threshold (column D). This pattern of disparity holds for blacks in all nine divisions, ranging from a low of 0.56 in the Mountain states to a high of 0.71 in the Pacific division. Moreover, column E shows that between 40 and 50 percent of the overall difference in self-employment rates between whites and blacks is attributable to discrimination, depending on geographic location.

A similar pattern of disparity is apparent for Hispanics as well. In seven of nine divisions, the disparity ratio in column D is substantially below the 80 percent threshold. Moreover, the portion of the self-employment difference attributable to discrimination is large as well, ranging between 36 and 65 percent (column E). Two divisions exhibit exceptions to this pattern. First, in the East South Central division, which accounts for less than 1 percent of all self-employed Hispanics in the U.S. (*see* Table 2.15), the observed Hispanic self-employment rate exceeds that for non-Hispanic whites. Second, in the South Atlantic division, which accounts for more than 20 percent of the self-employed Hispanic population in the U.S., the disparity ratio is 0.87, which is well above the 80 percent threshold for substantiality.

For Native Americans the results are more mixed. For example, Native Americans are found to have large adjusted disparities in three divisions (New England, Middle Atlantic, Mountain), moderate disparities in four divisions (Pacific, East North Central, West North Central, and West South Central), and no disparities in the remaining two divisions (South Atlantic and East South Central). In all but these last two divisions, a substantial portion of the difference in self-employment rates is also attributable to discrimination, as shown in column E.

In contrast to the results for blacks, Hispanics, and Native Americans, Asians appear to enjoy self-employment rates that are generally equivalent to or higher than corresponding non-Hispanic white rates. In six of the geographic divisions examined, Asians have higher self-

Table 3.3. Observed and adjusted self-employment rates for census divisions

Division/race group	Observed self-employment rate	White Characteristics and Own Market Structure	Own Characteristics and White Market Structure	Disparity Ratio (column A ÷ column C)	Portion of Difference Due to Discrimination
	(A)	(B)	(C)	(D)	(E)
New England					
white	0.150	0.150	0.150	1.000	
black	0.054	0.091	0.095	0.568	0.427
Hispanic	0.055	0.096	0.089	0.618	0.358
Asian	0.116	0.136	0.127	0.913	0.324
Native	0.051	0.058	0.137	0.372	0.869
Middle Atlantic					
white	0.153	0.153	0.153	1.000	
black	0.066	0.095	0.111	0.595	0.517
Hispanic	0.087	0.104	0.130	0.669	0.652
Asian	0.173	0.131	0.198	0.874	N/A
Native	0.082	0.104	0.124	0.661	0.592
East North Central					
white	0.115	0.115	0.115	1.000	
black	0.046	0.075	0.073	0.630	0.391
Hispanic	0.047	0.067	0.081	0.580	0.500
Asian	0.164	0.109	0.170	0.965	N/A
Native	0.071	0.098	0.084	0.845	0.295
West North Central					
white	0.130	0.130	0.130	1.000	
black	0.048	0.079	0.083	0.578	0.427
Hispanic	0.074	0.101	0.097	0.763	0.411
Asian	0.131	0.132	0.130	1.008	N/A
Native	0.098	0.125	0.103	0.951	0.156
South Atlantic					
white	0.154	0.154	0.154	1.000	
black	0.061	0.098	0.101	0.604	0.430
Hispanic	0.151	0.134	0.173	0.873	N/A
Asian	0.195	0.159	0.190	1.026	N/A
Native	0.144	0.157	0.141	1.021	N/A

East South Central					
white	0.139	0.139	0.139	1.000	
black	0.047	0.083	0.083	0.566	0.391
Hispanic	0.152	0.161	0.132	1.152	N/A
Asian	0.170	0.170	0.142	1.197	N/A
Native	0.131	0.148	0.122	1.074	N/A
West South Central					
white	0.158	0.158	0.158	1.000	
black	0.056	0.095	0.098	0.571	0.412
Hispanic	0.097	0.114	0.136	0.713	0.639
Asian	0.161	0.164	0.155	1.039	N/A
Native	0.119	0.149	0.127	0.937	0.205
Mountain					
white	0.153	0.153	0.153	1.000	
black	0.053	0.091	0.095	0.558	0.420
Hispanic	0.077	0.107	0.114	0.675	0.487
Asian	0.134	0.168	0.122	1.098	N/A
Native	0.077	0.110	0.111	0.694	0.447
Pacific					
white	0.175	0.175	0.175	1.000	
black	0.085	0.127	0.120	0.708	0.389
Hispanic	0.076	0.110	0.126	0.603	0.505
Asian	0.157	0.155	0.176	0.892	1.056
Native	0.108	0.146	0.133	0.812	0.373

Source: Author's calculations using Bureau of Census (1993).

employment rates than non-Hispanic whites. In the remaining three divisions (New England, Middle Atlantic, and Mountain) the disparity ratio for Asians, although less than one, exceeds the 80 percent substantiality threshold.

As a check on these findings, the final section of this study examines differences in the earnings of the self-employed to determine if similar patterns of racial and ethnic disadvantage are evident in this measure of entrepreneurial activity as well.

RESULTS OF BUSINESS EARNINGS ANALYSES

Three final tables present the results of the business earnings discrimination analysis. Table 3.4 presents the results of separate analyses con-

Table 3.4. Self-employment earnings decomposition results, by census division

Division/race group	$\ln(G_{wb}+1)$	$\ln(Q_{wb}+1)$	$\ln(D_{wb}+1)$	$\ln(D_{wo}+1)$	$\ln(D_{ob}+1)$
New England					
Black	0.1951**	0.1321**	0.063	0.0008	0.0622
	(0.0549)	(0.0127)	(0.0563)	(0.0114)	(0.0563)
Hispanic	0.2124**	0.1512**	0.0613	0.0007	0.0605
	(0.0572)	(0.0222)	(0.0613)	(0.0114)	(0.0612)
Asian	0.038	-0.0322	0.0701	0.0010	0.0692
	(0.0485)	(0.0289)	(0.0565)	(0.0114)	(0.0563)
Native[†]	0.1661**	0.0850**	0.0811**	0.000	0.0811**
	(0.0081)	(0.0187)	(0.0203)	(0.0114)	(0.0204)
Middle Atlantic					
Black	0.4623**	0.1703**	0.2919**	0.0114	0.2805**
	(0.0366)	(0.0085)	(0.0376)	(0.0076)	(0.0376)
Hispanic	0.4794**	0.3047**	0.1747**	0.0083	0.1664**
	(0.0255)	(0.0138)	(0.0290)	(0.0075)	(0.0287)
Asian	0.2557**	0.1494**	0.1062**	0.0049	0.1014**
	(0.0254)	(0.0164)	(0.0303)	(0.0075)	(0.0300)
Native	0.5346**	0.2595**	0.2751**	0.0002	0.2748**
	(0.0053)	(0.0089)	(0.0104)	(0.0076)	(0.0104)
East North Central					
Black	0.3917**	0.1368**	0.2549**	0.008	0.2469**
	(0.0424)	(0.0073)	(0.0430)	(0.0088)	(0.0431)
Hispanic	0.2277**	0.0707**	0.1570**	0.0024	0.1546**
	(0.0423)	(0.0171)	(0.0456)	(0.0088)	(0.0455)
Asian	-0.1931**	-0.2153**	0.0223	0.0005	0.0217
	(0.0308)	(0.0235)	(0.0387)	(0.0088)	(0.0382)
Native	0.4201**	0.2711**	0.1490**	0.0003	0.1488**
	(0.0281)	(0.0108)	(0.0301)	(0.0088)	(0.0302)
West North Central					
Black	0.3011**	0.0688**	0.2323**	0.0035	0.2289**
	(0.0740)	(0.0133)	(0.0752)	(0.0148)	(0.0751)
Hispanic	0.2304**	0.0559~	0.1745**	0.0014	0.1732**
	(0.0472)	(0.0336)	(0.0579)	(0.0147)	(0.0579)
Asian	0.0875	0.0093	0.0781	0.0007	0.0774
	(0.0709)	(0.0816)	(0.1080)	(0.0147)	(0.1079)
Native	0.4659**	0.2850**	0.1808**	0.0007	0.1801**
	(0.0232)	(0.0229)	(0.0326)	(0.0148)	(0.0325)
South Atlantic					
Black	0.3988**	0.1951**	0.2038**	0.0125	0.1913**
	(0.0261)	(0.0066)	(0.0269)	(0.0078)	(0.0268)
Hispanic	0.2348**	0.1766**	0.0582*	0.0037	0.0545*
	(0.0203)	(0.0153)	(0.0254)	(0.0078)	(0.0247)

Asian	0.0004	-0.0144	0.0147	0.0004	0.0144
	(0.0323)	(0.0213)	(0.0386)	(0.0079)	(0.0383)
Native	0.3780**	0.2075**	0.1705*	0.0006	0.1700*
	(0.0680)	(0.0055)	(0.0683)	(0.0079)	(0.0682)
East South Central					
Black	0.4905**	0.2701**	0.2203**	0.0098	0.2105**
	(0.0554)	(0.0168)	(0.0579)	(0.0160)	(0.0579)
Hispanic	0.1074**	0.0653~	0.0421	0.0002	0.0419
	(0.0185)	(0.0362)	(0.0407)	(0.0161)	(0.0404)
Asian	0.0755~	-0.0548	0.1303	0.001	0.1293
	(0.0429)	(0.0716)	(0.0834)	(0.0161)	(0.0827)
Native	0.5321**	0.0957**	0.4364**	0.0011	0.4354**
	(0.0114)	(0.0290)	(0.0312)	(0.0162)	(0.0305)
West South Central					
Black	0.4324**	0.2016**	0.2308**	0.0094	0.2214**
	(0.0389)	(0.0100)	(0.0401)	(0.0111)	(0.0400)
Hispanic	0.3808**	0.3018**	0.0790**	0.0083	0.0708**
	(0.0246)	(0.0141)	(0.0283)	(0.0110)	(0.0273)
Asian	0.1975**	0.0609	0.1367*	0.0034	0.1333*
	(0.0546)	(0.0400)	(0.0677)	(0.0112)	(0.0673)
Native	0.5073**	0.1836**	0.3238**	0.003	0.3207**
	(0.0907)	(0.0074)	(0.0910)	(0.0112)	(0.0910)
Mountain					
Black	0.4440**	0.2803**	0.1637**	0.0016	0.1621**
	(0.0588)	(0.0206)	(0.0623)	(0.0158)	(0.0623)
Hispanic	0.2068**	0.2150**	-0.0082	-0.0005	-0.0077
	(0.0400)	(0.0168)	(0.0434)	(0.0156)	(0.0428)
Asian	0.2916**	0.2696**	0.022	0.0004	0.0216
	(0.0632)	(0.0436)	(0.0768)	(0.0157)	(0.0764)
Native	0.3869**	0.0650**	0.3219**	0.0014	0.3205**
	(0.0178)	(0.0131)	(0.0221)	(0.0158)	(0.0217)
Pacific					
Black	0.2964**	0.1099**	0.1866**	0.005	0.1815**
	(0.0385)	(0.0055)	(0.0389)	(0.0082)	(0.0389)
Hispanic	0.4380**	0.3184**	0.1196**	0.0118	0.1078**
	(0.0183)	(0.0103)	(0.0210)	(0.0081)	(0.0205)
Asian	0.2074**	0.1553**	0.0521**	0.0057	0.0464*
	(0.0168)	(0.0111)	(0.0202)	(0.0081)	(0.0194)
Native	0.4438**	0.1697**	0.2740**	0.0014	0.2726**
	(0.0751)	(0.0061)	(0.0753)	(0.0082)	(0.0754)

Source: Author's calculations using Bureau of Census (1993).

Note: Standard errors in parentheses with p<0.10 = ~, p<0.05 = *, p<0.01 = **.

† Ten or fewer minority observations in sample.

ducted for each of the nine census geographic divisions. For each division, as described above in equations (9) through (20), separate earnings regressions were estimated for each of the five racial and ethnic groups included in the sample. Four pooled white-minority regressions were also estimated—one for each minority group in the sample. These regressions used the same set of explanatory variables as was used in the logit regression analyses presented earlier in this chapter, including control variables for industry and occupation.[81]

Tables 3.5 and 3.6 follow the same format as Table 3.4. The difference is that Table 3.5 is disaggregated by industry division rather than geographic division, while Table 3.6 is disaggregated by major occupation group rather than geographic division.[82] The first column in Tables 3.4, 3.5, and 3.6 contains the logarithm of the gross wage differential between non-Hispanic whites and each minority group, as defined above in equation (3). The second column contains the logarithm of that part of the gross differential that is estimated to be due to differences in individual characteristics between groups, defined above in equation (4). The third column is the logarithm of that part of the gross differential that is estimated to be due to differences in market structure, as defined above in equation (5). This is the measure of discrimination for this model. The fourth and fifth columns show that part of the discrimination differential which is due to overpayment of whites and that which is due to underpayment of blacks, respectively, defined above as in equation (7). Since non-Hispanic whites comprise a large majority of the sample in each division, the estimated non-discriminatory earnings structure is much closer to the white structure than it is to the minority structure. Consequently, most of the measured discrimination is attributable to underpayment of minorities.[83]

Geographic Analyses

The first column in Table 3.4 shows that the hourly earnings of self-employed minorities fall far below their non-Hispanic white counterparts in almost all instances. Black, Hispanic, and Native American entrepreneurs earn much less than non-Hispanic white entrepreneurs in all nine geographic divisions. The black earnings gap ranges from 20 percent in New England to 49 percent in the East South Central division. The Hispanic earnings gap ranges from 11 percent in the East South Central to 48 percent in the Middle Atlantic division. The Native American earnings gap ranges from 17 percent in New England to 53 percent in the Middle Atlantic and the East South Central divisions. Asian entrepreneurs earn less than white entrepreneurs in seven divisions, with the earnings gap ranging from a low of only 4 percent to a high of 29 percent.

It is clear from Table 3.4 that individual differences in economic and demographic attributes account for a substantial portion of this overall earnings gap between self-employed minorities and self-employed nonminorities. As column two shows, individual differences account for a large and statistically significant portion of the overall earnings gap for blacks, Hispanics, and Native Americans in all nine divisions, and for Asians in five divisions. However, Table 3.4 also shows that even when these substantial individual differences are accounted for, racial and ethnic self-employment earnings disparities are *still* observed. In most cases these disparities are both statistically significant and large in size.

This pattern is most pronounced for blacks. Positive amounts of discrimination are observed in eight of nine census divisions, ranging from 0.16 in the Mountain division to 0.29 in the Middle Atlantic, compared to gross differentials that range between 0.30 in the West North Central division and 0.49 in the East South Central. In other words, even after holding other economic and demographic characteristics constant, the (log) hourly earnings of self-employed blacks were 16 to 29 percent lower than those of non-Hispanic whites. Measured discrimination against blacks in these eight divisions accounts for between 37 percent and 77 percent of the total observed differential in wages, depending on division.[84] All eight of these disparities are statistically significant at better than a 1 percent level. The single exception to this pattern occurs in New England. The gross wage differential facing blacks in New England is 19.5 percent—the smallest in the nation. Here, measured discrimination accounts for only 6.3 percentage points of the wage difference, or 32 percent of the total. This figure is far below that observed elsewhere in the nation, and is not statistically significant.

For Hispanics, discrimination is observed in eight of nine divisions, and is statistically significant in six of nine divisions. Discriminatory earnings differentials range from about 5 percentage points of the overall gap in New England and in the East South Central division to about 17 percent in the Middle Atlantic and West North Central divisions. Discrimination accounts for 70 to 75 percent of the overall Hispanic earnings differential in the East North Central and West North Central divisions, and 20 to 40 percent of the overall differential elsewhere.

For Native Americans, the pattern is similar to that found for blacks. Measured discrimination against Native American entrepreneurs is substantial in all nine geographic divisions, ranging from a low of 8 percentage points in New England to a high of 44 percentage points in the East South Central states. Between 40 and 80 percent of the overall earnings gap for Native Americans, depending on geographic location, is therefore attributable to discrimination.

As documented earlier in this chapter, Asians as a group tend to have self-employment rates that are equal to or greater than those observed for non-Hispanic whites. With regard to hourly earnings, however, the same cannot be said. The earnings of self-employed Asians equal or exceed those of non-Hispanic whites in only two divisions, the East North Central and the South Atlantic. In the remaining divisions, the Asian earnings gap ranges from moderate (in New England, the West North Central, and the East South Central divisions) to severe (in the Middle Atlantic, West South Central, Mountain, and Pacific divisions). Positive levels of discrimination are observed for Asians in all nine geographic divisions, ranging across divisions from about 2 percentage points to 14 percentage points. These differences are statistically significant in three divisions (the Middle Atlantic, the West South Central, and the Pacific).

In summary, the results of a geographically disaggregated business earnings analysis show positive levels of measured discrimination in all nine divisions examined and for all four minority groups examined. Although a considerable portion of the gross wage differential for all minority groups is due to differences in individual characteristics, a large portion of the gap is almost always left unaccounted for. Thus, measured discrimination against minorities is apparent in almost all instances, and is substantial and statistically significant in the large majority of cases. Measured discrimination is most severe for blacks and Native Americans. Discrimination is evident against Hispanics and Asians as well, although at somewhat lower and more varied levels than observed for blacks and Native Americans.

As a check on the results obtained when disaggregating the PUMS sample by geographic division, I also checked for the presence of discriminatory earnings differentials when the sample data were disaggregated by industry division and by major occupation group. These results are presented below in Tables 3.5 and 3.6, respectively.

Industry Analyses

When racial and ethnic self-employment earnings differentials are examined according to industry division, large disparities are observed in almost every instance. For blacks, the earnings gap is smallest in the entertainment and recreation services industries (16.8 percent) and largest in manufacturing industries (53.7 percent). In the construction industries, which are often the focus of government affirmative action programs for minority business enterprises, the earnings gap for blacks is 32.0 percent. For Hispanics, the gap is smallest in personal services industries (16.9 percent) and largest in the mining industries (45.9 percent). In construction, the Hispanic earnings gap is 26.6 percent.

For Native Americans, the overall earnings gap is smallest in the business and repair services industries (17.4 percent) and largest in the wholesale trade industries (75.6 percent).[85] In construction the Native American entrepreneurial earnings gap is 38.3 percent. Black, Hispanic, and Native American earnings gaps are highly statistically significant in all eleven industry divisions.

Asians face overall earnings gaps in seven of ten industry divisions, ranging from 6.4 percent in the personal services industries to 21.6 percent in the transportation industries.[86] These differences are statistically significant in six of these seven divisions. In three other divisions, Asian entrepreneurs earn more per hour than their non-Hispanic white counterparts (professional and related services, business and repair services, and construction).

In every industry division examined, positive levels of discrimination are observed for all four minority groups. For blacks, the discrimination gap ranges from a low of 6.4 percentage points in the entertainment and recreation services industries to 42.1 percentage points in the mining industries. Measured discrimination for blacks is statistically significant in ten of eleven industry divisions, the sole exception being entertainment and recreational services. In the construction industries, discrimination accounts for 24.5 percentage points of the earnings gap. Expressed as a percentage of the total self-employed earnings gap, discrimination is responsible for between approximately 40 percent and 80 percent of this gap, depending on industry division.

For Hispanics, the discrimination gap is lowest, at 3.8 percentage points, in the finance, insurance, and real estate industries. Measured discrimination is at its highest—26.4 percent—in the mining industries. In construction, the discrimination gap for Hispanics is 12.0 percentage points. These figures are statistically significant in seven of eleven industry divisions. Overall, discrimination accounts for between about 20 percent and 60 percent of the overall earnings gap facing Hispanics, depending on industry division.

Discrimination against Native American business owners is observed in all eleven industry divisions examined and is statistically significant in ten. No significant amount of discrimination is observed in the business and repair services industries. In other industries, however, discrimination is prominent. At its lowest, discrimination accounts for 17.2 percentage points of the overall earnings gap in the manufacturing industries. At its highest, discrimination accounts for 36.6 percentage points of the Native American earnings gap in the wholesale trade industries. Overall, discrimination accounts for between about 15 percent and 90 percent of the overall earnings gap facing Native Americans.

Asians face positive levels of discrimination in nine of ten industry divisions examined, four of which are statistically significant. Discrimination against Asians even shows up in two of the three industry divisions in which there is no overall Asian-white earnings gap. For example, column one of Table 3.5 shows that Asians enjoy a 4.1 percent earnings advantage in the construction industries over non-Hispanic whites. Examination of the corresponding values in column two and column three of the table show that, on average, Asians in the construction industries are more "qualified" than non-Hispanic whites and that, but-for discrimination, Asians would be expected to earn almost 15 percent more than non-Hispanic whites in the construction industries.[87]

In summary, the results in Table 3.5 suggest that there is substantial racial and ethnic discrimination evident when the earnings of similarly situated minorities and non-minorities are compared within each of eleven major industry categories. Overall earnings gaps are quite large and usually statistically significant. A substantial percentage of this gap is generally left unaccounted for even after a wide variety of individual economic and demographic characteristics are held constant.

Occupational Analyses

Finally, I examined racial and ethnic self-employment earnings differentials according to major occupation group, and again found large disparities in most cases. Earnings differentials are observed for blacks in all occupational groups except technicians and related occupations. Elsewhere, the black business earnings gap ranges from 16.9 percent below corresponding white earnings (in transportation and material moving occupations) to 43.0 percent below white earnings (in farming, forestry, and fishing occupations). For Hispanics, earnings disadvantages are observed in all occupational groups except protective services. Hispanic

Table 3.5. Self-employment earnings decomposition results, by industry division

Division/race group	$\ln(G_{wb}+1)$	$\ln(Q_{wb}+1)$	$\ln(D_{wb}+1)$	$\ln(D_{wo}+1)$	$\ln(D_{ob}+1)$
Mining					
Black[†]	0.5166**	0.0960	0.4206**	0.0056	0.4150**
	(0.0395)	(0.1571)	(0.1620)	(0.0559)	(0.1580)
Hispanic	0.4586**	0.1951	0.2635~	0.0040	0.2595~
	(0.0395)	(0.1542)	(0.1592)	(0.0559)	(0.1514)
Asian[††]	N/A	N/A	N/A	N/A	N/A
	N/A	N/A	N/A	N/A	N/A
Native[†]	0.2046**	-0.0514	0.2560**	0.0028	0.2532**
	(0.0395)	(0.0741)	(0.0840)	(0.0561)	(0.0856)
Construction					
Black	0.3199**	0.0747**	0.2451**	0.0082	0.2370**
	(0.0328)	(0.0055)	(0.0333)	(0.0069)	(0.0333)
Hispanic	0.2660**	0.1461**	0.1199**	0.0065	0.1134**
	(0.0222)	(0.0112)	(0.0249)	(0.0069)	(0.0246)
Asian	-0.0410	-0.1475**	0.1065*	0.0012	0.1052*
	(0.0414)	(0.0205)	(0.0462)	(0.0069)	(0.0461)
Native	0.3828**	0.0658**	0.3170**	0.0015	0.3155**
	(0.0886)	(0.0054)	(0.0888)	(0.0069)	(0.0888)
Manufacturing					
Black	0.5365**	0.2522**	0.2843**	0.0063	0.2780**
	(0.0565)	(0.0108)	(0.0575)	(0.0115)	(0.0575)
Hispanic	0.4201**	0.2643**	0.1559**	0.0089	0.1470**
	(0.0369)	(0.0227)	(0.0433)	(0.0115)	(0.0429)
Asian	0.0655~	0.0221	0.0435	0.0014	0.0421
	(0.0390)	(0.0281)	(0.0480)	(0.0115)	(0.0476)
Native	0.2883**	0.1162**	0.1721*	0.0007	0.1713*
	(0.0771)	(0.0128)	(0.0781)	(0.0115)	(0.0781)
Transportation, communications, and public utilities					
Black	0.2916**	0.1557**	0.1358**	0.0148	0.1210**
	(0.0388)	(0.0141)	(0.0413)	(0.0164)	(0.0407)
Hispanic	0.2072**	0.1578**	0.0494	0.0046	0.0448
	(0.0390)	(0.0257)	(0.0467)	(0.0165)	(0.0454)
Asian	0.2162**	0.1277**	0.0884	0.0030	0.0854
	(0.0546)	(0.0442)	(0.0703)	(0.0166)	(0.0697)
Native	0.3302**	0.0888**	0.2414**	0.0013	0.2401**
	(0.0762)	(0.0141)	(0.0775)	(0.0167)	(0.0776)

Table 3.5. Self-employment earnings decomposition results, by industry division (*cont.*)

Division/race group	$\ln(G_{wb}+1)$	$\ln(Q_{wb}+1)$	$\ln(D_{wb}+1)$	$\ln(D_{wo}+1)$	$\ln(D_{ob}+1)$
Wholesale trade					
Black	0.4649**	0.1998**	0.2651**	0.0048	0.2602**
	(0.0680)	(0.0146)	(0.0695)	(0.0127)	(0.0696)
Hispanic	0.4068**	0.3132**	0.0936~	0.0051	0.0886~
	(0.0407)	(0.0255)	(0.0480)	(0.0127)	(0.0475)
Asian	0.1174**	0.0143	0.1032~	0.0043	0.0989~
	(0.0445)	(0.0295)	(0.0534)	(0.0127)	(0.0528)
Native	0.7557**	0.3900**	0.3657**	0.0008	0.3649**
	(0.0090)	(0.0185)	(0.0206)	(0.0128)	(0.0209)
Retail trade					
Black	0.3190**	0.0662**	0.2528**	0.0070	0.2458**
	(0.0478)	(0.0057)	(0.0481)	(0.0085)	(0.0481)
Hispanic	0.2525**	0.1419**	0.1106**	0.0074	0.1031**
	(0.0207)	(0.0112)	(0.0236)	(0.0084)	(0.0229)
Asian	0.1899**	0.0948**	0.0951**	0.0079	0.0872**
	(0.0204)	(0.0144)	(0.0250)	(0.0084)	(0.0242)
Native	0.4362**	0.1722**	0.2640**	0.0008	0.2632**
	(0.0680)	(0.0062)	(0.0683)	(0.0085)	(0.0684)
Finance, insurance, and real estate					
Black	0.3706**	0.1051**	0.2656**	0.0076	0.2579**
	(0.0488)	(0.0086)	(0.0496)	(0.0123)	(0.0495)
Hispanic	0.1980**	0.1598**	0.0382	0.0012	0.037
	(0.0425)	(0.0205)	(0.0472)	(0.0123)	(0.0468)
Asian	0.1886**	-0.0292	0.2178**	0.0064	0.2114**
	(0.0487)	(0.0300)	(0.0572)	(0.0123)	(0.0567)
Native	0.5076**	0.2974**	0.2102**	0.0004	0.2098**
	(0.0087)	(0.0202)	(0.0220)	(0.0124)	(0.0220)
Business and repair services					
Black	0.2569**	0.1059**	0.1510**	0.0072	0.1438**
	(0.0334)	(0.0078)	(0.0343)	(0.0102)	(0.0341)
Hispanic	0.2376**	0.1743**	0.0633*	0.0045	0.0588*
	(0.0250)	(0.0155)	(0.0294)	(0.0101)	(0.0287)
Asian	-0.1204**	-0.1283**	0.0078	0.0002	0.0076
	(0.0360)	(0.0231)	(0.0428)	(0.0102)	(0.0424)
Native	0.1739**	0.1484**	0.0256	0.0001	0.0255
	(0.0502)	(0.0094)	(0.0511)	(0.0102)	(0.0511)

Personal services					
Black	0.2917**	0.0715**	0.2202**	0.0157	0.2045**
	(0.0549)	(0.0138)	(0.0566)	(0.0194)	(0.0559)
Hispanic	0.1689**	0.1158**	0.0531	0.0042	0.0489
	(0.0448)	(0.0216)	(0.0497)	(0.0192)	(0.0486)
Asian	0.0637	0.0517	0.0119	0.0012	0.0108
	(0.0405)	(0.0325)	(0.0519)	(0.0193)	(0.0497)
Native	0.3827**	0.0538	0.3289**	0.0009	0.3280**
	(0.0138)	(0.0359)	(0.0384)	(0.0195)	(0.0385)
Entertainment and recreational services					
Black	0.1683*	0.1048**	0.0635	0.0028	0.0607
	(0.0846)	(0.0208)	(0.0871)	(0.0290)	(0.0875)
Hispanic	0.3148**	0.2261**	0.0887	0.0044	0.0843
	(0.0708)	(0.0539)	(0.0890)	(0.0290)	(0.0877)
Asian	0.1671*	0.0585	0.1086	0.0031	0.1055
	(0.0694)	(0.0663)	(0.0960)	(0.0291)	(0.0947)
Native[†]	0.9689**	0.2323**	0.7366**	0.0028	0.7338**
	(0.0207)	(0.0589)	(0.0624)	(0.0293)	(0.0633)
Professional and related services					
Black	0.4634**	0.2442**	0.2192**	0.006	0.2132**
	(0.0376)	(0.0067)	(0.0382)	(0.0073)	(0.0383)
Hispanic	0.2034**	0.1377**	0.0657*	0.0022	0.0634*
	(0.0272)	(0.0121)	(0.0297)	(0.0072)	(0.0296)
Asian	-0.1405**	-0.1401**	-0.0004	0.0000	-0.0004
	(0.0223)	(0.0148)	(0.0268)	(0.0072)	(0.0263)
Native	0.6623**	0.3560**	0.3063**	0.0007	0.3056**
	(0.0738)	(0.0079)	(0.0742)	(0.0073)	(0.0743)

Source: Author's calculations using Bureau of Census (1993).
Note: Standard errors in parentheses with $p<0.10 = \sim$, $p<0.05 = *$, $p<0.01 = **$.
† Ten or fewer minority observations in sample. †† Not enough information available to calculate results.

earnings gaps in the remaining occupational categories range from 10.3 percent to 40.0 percent below corresponding levels for non-Hispanic whites. Native Americans entrepreneurs appear to earn the same or slightly more than non-Hispanic whites in three of ten occupational groups examined, and significantly less than whites in the seven others.[88] Asians enjoy earnings advantages in six occupational groups and suffer disadvantages in six others.

To avoid repetition and save space, I leave it to the interested reader as an exercise to verify that substantial and statistically significant evi-

Table 3.6. Self-employment earnings decomposition results, by major occupation group

Division/race group	$\ln(G_{wb}+1)$	$\ln(Q_{wb}+1)$	$\ln(D_{wb}+1)$	$\ln(D_{wo}+1)$	$\ln(D_{ob}+1)$
Executive, administrative, and managerial occupations					
Black	0.3884**	0.1237**	0.2646**	0.0072	0.2575**
	(0.0383)	(0.0048)	(0.0386)	(0.0071)	(0.0386)
Hispanic	0.3109**	0.2008**	0.1101**	0.0047	0.1054**
	(0.0244)	(0.0109)	(0.0267)	(0.0070)	(0.0265)
Asian	0.2768**	0.1649**	0.1120**	0.005	0.1069**
	(0.0243)	(0.0152)	(0.0287)	(0.0070)	(0.0284)
Native	0.4294**	0.1478**	0.2815**	0.001	0.2805**
	(0.0675)	(0.0055)	(0.0677)	(0.0071)	(0.0677)
Professional specialty occupations					
Black	0.3691**	0.1682**	0.2009**	0.0048	0.1960**
	(0.0427)	(0.0056)	(0.0430)	(0.0076)	(0.0431)
Hispanic	0.1650**	0.0895**	0.0755*	0.0025	0.0730*
	(0.0283)	(0.0127)	(0.0310)	(0.0076)	(0.0308)
Asian	-0.1832**	-0.1852**	0.002	0.0001	0.0019
	(0.0228)	(0.0150)	(0.0273)	(0.0076)	(0.0268)
Native	0.7302**	0.3092**	0.4210**	0.0009	0.4201**
	(0.0812)	(0.0088)	(0.0817)	(0.0076)	(0.0818)
Technicians and related support occupations					
Black	0.0062	-0.0217	0.0279	0.0008	0.0271
	(0.0543)	(0.0253)	(0.0599)	(0.0294)	(0.0584)
Hispanic	0.1025~	-0.0066	0.1091~	0.0045	0.1046~
	(0.0523)	(0.0362)	(0.0636)	(0.0294)	(0.0605)
Asian	-0.1592**	-0.1946**	0.0354	0.0015	0.0339
	(0.0595)	(0.0495)	(0.0774)	(0.0294)	(0.0746)
Native†	-0.0177	-0.1242*	0.1065	0.0003	0.1061~
	(0.0209)	(0.0623)	(0.0657)	(0.0296)	(0.0636)
Sales occupations					
Black	0.3678**	0.0881**	0.2797**	0.0064	0.2733**
	(0.0405)	(0.0051)	(0.0408)	(0.0075)	(0.0408)
Hispanic	0.3328**	0.2469**	0.0859**	0.004	0.0819**
	(0.0223)	(0.0129)	(0.0257)	(0.0074)	(0.0253)
Asian	0.2781**	0.1837**	0.0944**	0.0047	0.0897**
	(0.0227)	(0.0159)	(0.0277)	(0.0075)	(0.0272)
Native	0.6302**	0.2828**	0.3475**	0.0008	0.3466**
	(0.0921)	(0.0074)	(0.0924)	(0.0075)	(0.0924)

Administrative support occupations

Black	0.4054**	0.0862**	0.3192**	0.0162	0.3031**
	(0.0637)	(0.0260)	(0.0688)	(0.0267)	(0.0677)
Hispanic	0.1942**	0.1439**	0.0503	0.0032	0.047
	(0.0487)	(0.0371)	(0.0612)	(0.0266)	(0.0581)
Asian	0.1416*	0.1246*	0.017	0.0007	0.0163
	(0.0572)	(0.0502)	(0.0761)	(0.0266)	(0.0744)
Native††	N/A	N/A	N/A	N/A	N/A
	N/A	N/A	N/A	N/A	N/A

Protective service occupations

Black	0.3785**	0.0724	0.3061**	0.026	0.2801**
	(0.0449)	(0.0745)	(0.0870)	(0.0636)	(0.0831)
Hispanic	-0.0731	-0.0884	0.0154	0.0009	0.0144
	(0.0449)	(0.0818)	(0.0933)	(0.0631)	(0.0828)
Asian†	-0.3232**	-0.1226	-0.2006	-0.0039	-0.1967
	(0.0449)	(0.1182)	(0.1264)	(0.0630)	(0.1228)
Native††	N/A	N/A	N/A	N/A	N/A
	N/A	N/A	N/A	N/A	N/A

Other service occupations

Black	0.1783**	0.016	0.1623**	0.0172	0.1451**
	(0.0448)	(0.0120)	(0.0464)	(0.0180)	(0.0460)
Hispanic	0.1035**	0.0521**	0.0515	0.0062	0.0452
	(0.0351)	(0.0192)	(0.0400)	(0.0179)	(0.0384)
Asian	0.1903**	0.1487**	0.0416	0.0039	0.0377
	(0.0364)	(0.0298)	(0.0471)	(0.0181)	(0.0447)
Native	0.2203**	0.0577*	0.1626**	0.0011	0.1615**
	(0.0226)	(0.0232)	(0.0324)	(0.0182)	(0.0333)

Farming, forestry, and fishing

Black	0.4302**	0.1736~	0.2566~	0.0119	0.2447~
	(0.0976)	(0.0909)	(0.1334)	(0.0524)	(0.1264)
Hispanic	0.3990**	0.1790~	0.2200*	0.0099	0.2101*
	(0.0366)	(0.1024)	(0.1087)	(0.0514)	(0.1035)
Asian†	-0.2804**	-0.4013**	0.1209	0.0017	0.1192
	(0.0366)	(0.1502)	(0.1546)	(0.0517)	(0.1487)
Native†	-0.0935*	-0.0999	0.0063	0.0001	0.0063
	(0.0366)	(0.0966)	(0.1033)	(0.0515)	(0.1068)

Construction trades

Black	0.2600**	0.0624**	0.1976**	0.007	0.1906**
	(0.0358)	(0.0063)	(0.0364)	(0.0080)	(0.0363)
Hispanic	0.2531**	0.1227**	0.1304**	0.008	0.1224**
	(0.0248)	(0.0132)	(0.0281)	(0.0080)	(0.0277)
Asian	-0.0476	-0.1205**	0.0729	0.0008	0.0721
	(0.0466)	(0.0277)	(0.0543)	(0.0080)	(0.0542)

Table 3.6. Self-employment earnings decomposition results, by major occupation group

Division/race group	$\ln(G_{wb}+1)$	$\ln(Q_{wb}+1)$	$\ln(D_{wb}+1)$	$\ln(D_{wo}+1)$	$\ln(D_{ob}+1)$
Native	0.2690**	0.0826**	0.1865*	0.0009	0.1856*
	(0.0776)	(0.0068)	(0.0779)	(0.0080)	(0.0779)
Precision production and craft occupations					
Black	0.2927**	0.0711**	0.2216**	0.008	0.2136**
	(0.0454)	(0.0081)	(0.0461)	(0.0108)	(0.0460)
Hispanic	0.1723**	0.0822**	0.0901**	0.0072	0.0829**
	(0.0273)	(0.0166)	(0.0320)	(0.0107)	(0.0313)
Asian	-0.0759~	-0.0971**	0.0212	0.0007	0.0205
	(0.0395)	(0.0252)	(0.0468)	(0.0108)	(0.0464)
Native	-0.0314	0.0265*	-0.058	-0.0002	-0.0578
	(0.0573)	(0.0113)	(0.0584)	(0.0108)	(0.0584)
Operators, fabricators, and laborers					
Black	0.2971**	0.0273~	0.2698**	0.0103	0.2595**
	(0.0798)	(0.0152)	(0.0813)	(0.0218)	(0.0812)
Hispanic	0.2829**	0.1548**	0.1280~	0.0122	0.1158~
	(0.0544)	(0.0376)	(0.0661)	(0.0216)	(0.0649)
Asian	0.0862	0.0656	0.0205	0.001	0.0196
	(0.0550)	(0.0502)	(0.0745)	(0.0217)	(0.0731)
Native	0.2783**	0.1484**	0.1298**	0.0006	0.1292**
	(0.0155)	(0.0312)	(0.0348)	(0.0219)	(0.0349)
Transportation & material moving occupations					
Black	0.1687**	0.0594**	0.1093**	0.0127	0.0966**
	(0.0340)	(0.0138)	(0.0367)	(0.0162)	(0.0359)
Hispanic	0.1792**	0.1404**	0.0389	0.0039	0.035
	(0.0359)	(0.0258)	(0.0442)	(0.0164)	(0.0427)
Asian	0.2156**	0.1627**	0.053	0.0014	0.0515
	(0.0572)	(0.0481)	(0.0747)	(0.0165)	(0.0742)
Native	0.2544**	0.0446**	0.2098**	0.0013	0.2085**
	(0.0657)	(0.0141)	(0.0672)	(0.0166)	(0.0672)

Source: Author's calculations using Bureau of Census (1993).
Note: Standard errors in parentheses with p<0.10 = ~, p<0.05 = *, p<0.01 = **.
† Ten or fewer minority observations in sample. †† Not enough information available to calculate results.

dence of discrimination is apparent for blacks in eleven of twelve occupational groups, for Hispanics in eight of twelve groups, for Native Americans in eight of ten groups, and for Asians in two groups.

In summary, Table 3.6 shows that substantial racial and ethnic discrimination is evident when the earnings of similarly situated minorities and non-minorities are compared within each of twelve major occupational groups. For blacks, Hispanics, and Native Americans, overall earnings gaps are almost always large and almost always statistically significant. As with geography and industry, in almost all cases a substantial portion of this gap cannot be attributed to differences between minorities and non-minorities in individual economic and demographic attributes. Subject to the several caveats I have expressed along the way, I take this as evidence of racial and ethnic business discrimination.

CONCLUSION

The self-employed represent an important and growing sector of the economy. Among prime working age males, being an entrepreneur is a relatively more lucrative form of employment, on average, than working for a wage. Typically, however, non-Hispanic whites become entrepreneurs at much higher rates than minorities. Moreover, self-employed non-Hispanic whites receive much higher average earnings than their black, Hispanic, and Native American counterparts. In an attempt to respond to such inequalities numerous federal agencies, state agencies, cities, counties, and special districts have adopted affirmative action policies designed to increase the participation of minority business enterprises in public contracting and procurement processes. A series of U.S. Supreme Court decisions beginning in 1989, however, left the continued constitutionality of such affirmative action policies contingent upon detailed documentation by individual public entities of the continued existence of racial and ethnic discrimination against the self-employed in their own jurisdictions. At the time these court decisions were handed down, this was something few jurisdictions were in a position to do.

In contrast to salary and wage workers, the issue of racial and ethnic discrimination against such self-employed business owners has received little attention from economists. Those who have examined the issue discovered that most U.S. minority groups are severely disadvantaged in the realm of business enterprise activity.

Using a very large sample of 1990 census microdata, this book has documented for the first time the large disparities in business formation and earnings facing minority businesses across a wide variety of geographic locations, industry divisions, and occupational groups. Moreover, this book has demonstrated that these disparities tend to persist even when education, age, marital status, assets, industry, occupation and numerous other influential factors are held constant. The statistical findings are strongest for blacks, followed closely by Native Americans and Hispanics. Positive levels of discrimination are documented for Asians as well in many instances.

It is harmful to any democratic society if substantial segments of the population are prevented from engaging in or prospering from business enterprise activity because of discrimination. Although one can quibble with the particular choices I have made in this study regarding sample selection, explanatory variables, regression specifications, and the like, it should nevertheless give pause to even the staunchest critics of affirmative action in government contracting that so many large and statistically significant racial and ethnic business disparities are found to exist even when comparisons are restricted to similarly situated business owners.

NOTES

[50] A recent "Annals of Econometrics" volume of the *Journal of Econometrics* was devoted in its entirety to the econometrics of labor market segregation and discrimination. See Neuman and Silber (1994) for an introduction and overview.

[51] Exceptions are the first State of Louisiana Study (Lunn and Perry 1993), and post-1993 studies by National Economic Research Associates, Inc. (*e.g.* NERA 1994).

[52] Nevertheless, even the PUMS may buckle under the evidentiary burden imposed by the Supreme Court. The self-employed constitute less than fifteen percent of the labor force. Each minority group under consideration typically constitutes less—sometimes far less—than fifteen percent of the labor force. Considering that the PUMS is only a five percent sample to start with, the precision of the estimates will tend to decline in proportion to the number of dimensions of disaggregation as well as to the degree of disaggregation within each dimension.

[53] All these inquiries, however, used different data source and asset measures and employed differing model specifications. Consequently, as Fairlie and Meyer (1994, 13) note, they are not readily reconciled.

[54] I address here only these supply-side aspects. Modeling demand-side characteristics is outside the scope of the present inquiry, although several variables measuring macroeconomic conditions in metropolitan labor markets are included in the analyses in this chapter.

[55] These data limitations were discussed in chapter two.

[56] Compare, for example, *Concrete Works of Colorado, Inc. v. City and County of Denver*, 36 F.3d 1513 (10th Cir. 1994) with *Engineering Contractors Association of South Florida v. Metropolitan Dade County*, 122 F.3d 895 (11th Cir. 1997).

[57] All of the regression analyses performed in this study were carried out using Stata® statistical software (version 6). Stata® includes a large and growing suite of estimation commands devoted to the analysis of survey data.

[58] See Gastwirth (1988, 206–210) for more on the odds ratio and other methods for assessing differences between proportions. Mathematically, the formula for the odds ratio (OR) is:

$$OR = \frac{\text{success rate in group I}}{\text{success rate in group II}} \times \frac{\text{failure rate in group II}}{\text{failure rate in group I}}$$

[59] If the probit model were employed instead of the logit, the formula for this adjustment would be $P_j^a = 1 \Big/ \left[n_a \sum_{i=1}^{n_a} \Phi(x_{wi}\hat{b} + \hat{a}_j) \right]$, where $\Phi(.)$ is the cumulative function of the standard normal distribution.

[60] If the probit model were employed instead of the logit, the formula for this adjustment would be $P_j^b = 1 \Big/ n_b \sum_{i=1}^{n_b} \Phi\left(x_{ij}\hat{b}_w\right)$.

[61] This technique had appeared previously in the demography literature (Kitigawa 1955) and the sociology literature (Duncan 1968; Althauser and Wigler 1972).

[62] The model presented in this section is drawn from Oaxaca and Ransom (1994) and Neumark (1988).

[63] As will be seen below, because the wage regressions are specified as semilogarithmic, the term "average" used here is taken to refer to geometric mean wages rather than arithmetic mean wages. That is,

$$\overline{w} = \exp\left\{\left[\sum_{i=1}^{n} \ln(w_i)\right] \Big/ n\right\}$$

[64] I am abstracting for the moment from considerations of which independent variables belong on the right hand side of the wage equations. The particular specification of the variables in the log wage equations is discussed below.

[65] For discrimination or nepotism to exist in this model, marginal utility must be strictly decreasing for at least one type of black labor or be strictly increasing for at least one type of white labor.

[66] Since the model is cast in log-linear terms, and since it is possible for the self-employed to have negative earnings, I have reset the earnings of such individuals to zero rather than discard them. This is a weakness of the log-wage

model that is not present in the case of wage and salary workers. Others who have studied self-employment earnings have also faced with this problem (Borjas and Bronars 1989; Fairlie and Meyer 1996).

[67] The standard age minus schooling minus six formulation for potential experience yields negative values in certain cases. To avoid this difficulty an alternative specification was introduced by Welch (Willis 1986, 538). In Welch's version, potential experience is set to schooling minus 16 for those with less than a high school diploma, age minus 17 for high school graduates, age minus 19 for those with some college but without a bachelor's degree, and age minus 22 for those with a college degree or higher.

[68] The only exception was the inclusion of variables measuring local area macroeconomic conditions, discussed below.

[69] Cain (1986, 750–52, 760) has surveyed a large number of discrimination studies conducted in the 1960s and 1970s and documented the different explanatory variables employed in different studies. Aronson (1989) discusses the influence of many of these variables on the self-employment decision.

[70] The MABLE/Geocorr geographic correspondence engine can generate files showing the relationships between the basic PUMS geographic unit (the PUMA) and other types of geographic designations, including Primary Metropolitan Statistical Areas (PMSA) and Consolidated Metropolitan Statistical Areas (CMSA).

[71] Standard errors are expressed in terms of the untransformed logit regession coefficients. The adjusted Wald statistic is the complex survey data analogue of the likelihood ratio chi-squared test for the joint significance of all estimated coefficients (Eltinge and Sribney 1996).

[72] Professional degrees include, but are not necessarily limited to, "medicine, dentistry, chiropractic, optometry, osteopathic medicine, pharmacy, podiatry, veterinary medicine, law, and theology (Census Bureau 1992a, B-5).

[73] *See* equation (1), above.

[74] This is directly analogous to the method described above in equation (13), with $\hat{b}_o = \hat{b}_b$

[75] Standard errors for these adjusted probabilities, although not reported here, were estimated using the delta method. These estimated standard errors are very similar to those reported in Table 2.15 for observed self-employment rates.

[76] *See* equation (2), above.

[77] This is directly analogous to the method described above in equation (13), with $\hat{b}_o = \hat{b}_w$

[78] As discussed earlier in this chapter, the portion of a disparity that is due to discrimination will differ depending on whether the white wage structure, or the black wage structure, or something in between is adopted as the "no-discrimina-

tion" wage structure. The measures appearing in column B of Table 3.3 use the black wage structure to normalize the difference while the measures in column C, D, and E use the white wage structure.

[79] These rates correspond to those reported in Table 2.15, above.

[80] Although the two are closely related, the adjusted disparity ratios in column D are slightly different from the odds ratios (which I have also referred to as adjusted disparity ratios) appearing in Tables 3.1 and 3.2 . The odds ratio-based disparity ratio is formed by dividing the conditional probability of self-employment for a given minority group by the conditional probability of self-employment for non-minorities. The adjusted disparity ratio of column D is formed by dividing the conditional probability of minority self-employment by the conditional probability predicted if minorities faced the estimated coefficient vector for whites.

[81] The complete results from these regressions are not presented here due to space (not to mention aesthetic) considerations.

[82] Since Table 3.5 is disaggregated by industry, the indicator variables for industry obviously had to be excluded from the model. The occupational control variables were retained, however, and a set of indicator variables for geographic division was added as well. Similarly for Table 3.6, the occupational indicator variables were not included in the underlying regressions, but the industry variables were retained, and indicator variables for geographic division were added.

[83] Standard errors for columns one through five were estimated using the delta method of approximation.

[84] These figures are obtained by dividing the figure in column three by the corresponding figure in column one.

[85] The gap for Native Americans in the entertainment and recreation services industries, at 96.9 percent, is higher. However, this result is based on a subsample that includes ten or fewer self-employed Native Americans and probably isn't very reliable.

[86] Results for Asians in the mining industries are not available because of sample size restrictions.

[87] That is, the 4.1 percent earnings advantage listed in column one is equal to the 14.75 percent earnings advantage indicated in column two less the 10.65 percent earnings disadvantage indicated in column three.

[88] For two groups, administrative occupations and protective services occupations, sample sizes were too small to render usable results.

Works Cited

Abrams, Willie, and Dennis Courtland Hayes. 1990. A proposed minority business utilization ordinance. In U.S. Congress, House, Committee on the Judiciary, *Minority business set-aside programs: The City of Richmond v. J. A. Croson Company: A collection of articles by constitutional scholars and economists*, 73–78. 101st Cong., 1st sess., January.

Althauser, Robert P., and Michael Wigler. 1972. Standardization and component analysis. *Sociological Methods and Research* 1:97–135.

Areen, Judith C., and others. 1990. Constitutional scholars' statement on affirmative action after *City of Richmond v. J. A. Croson*. In U.S. Congress, House, Committee on the Judiciary, *Minority business set-aside programs: The City of Richmond v. J. A. Croson Company: A collection of articles by constitutional scholars and economists*, 9–12. 101st Cong., 1st sess., January.

Aronson Robert L. 1991. *Self-employment: A labor market perspective*. Ithaca, N.Y.: ILR Press.

Arrow, Kenneth. 1972a. Models of job discrimination. In *Racial discrimination in economic life*, ed. Anthony H. Pascal, 83–102. Lexington, Mass.: D.C. Heath and Company.

———. 1972b. Some mathematical models of race in the labor market. In *Racial discrimination in economic life*, ed. Anthony H. Pascal, 187–204. Lexington, Mass.: D.C. Heath and Company.

Ashenfelter, Orley. 1972. Racial discrimination and trade unions. *Journal of Political Economy* 80: 435–464.

Ashenfelter, Orley, and Ronald Oaxaca. 1987. The economics of discrimination: Economists enter the courtroom. *American Economic Review* 77: 321–325.

141

Barringer, Herbert, Robert W. Gardner, and Michael J. Levin. 1993. *Asians and Pacific Islanders in the United States*. New York: Russell Sage Foundation.

Bates, Timothy. 1988. *An analysis of income differentials among self-employed minorities*. Los Angeles: The UCLA Center for Afro-American Studies.

———. 1993. *Major studies of minority business*. Washington, D.C.: Joint Center for Political and Economic Studies Press.

Bean, Frank D., and Marta Tienda. 1987. *The Hispanic population of the United States*. New York: Russell Sage Foundation.

Bearse, Peter J. 1984. An econometric analysis of black entrepreneurship. *Review of Black Political Economy* 12: 111–134.

Becker, Gary. [1957] 1971. *The economics of discrimination*. Chicago: University of Chicago Press.

Bendick, Marc Jr. 1990. The *Croson* decision mandates that set-aside programs be tools of business development. In U.S. Congress, House, Committee on the Judiciary, *Minority business set-aside programs: The City of Richmond v. J. A. Croson Company: A collection of articles by constitutional scholars and economists*, 93–109. 101st Cong., 1st sess., January.

Benjamin, Joyce Holmes. 1990. The Supreme Court decision and the future of race-conscious remedies. In U.S. Congress, House, Committee on the Judiciary, *Minority business set-aside programs: The City of Richmond v. J. A. Croson Company: A collection of articles by constitutional scholars and economists*, 65–72. 101st Cong., 1st sess., January.

Bernhardt, Irwin. 1994. Comparative advantage in self-employment and work. *Canadian Journal of Economics* 27: 273–289.

Blanchflower, David G., and Andrew J. Oswald. 1990. What makes an entrepreneur. Working Paper, Department of Economics, Dartmouth College.

Blaug, Mark. 1985. *Economic theory in retrospect*. Cambridge: Cambridge University Press.

Blinder, Alan S. 1973. Wage discrimination: Reduced form and structural estimates. *Journal of Human Resources* 8: 436–455.

Bloom, David E., and Mark R. Killingsworth. 1982. Pay discrimination research and litigation: The use of regression. *Industrial Relations* 21: 318–339.

Borjas, George J. 1986. The self-employment experience of immigrants. *Journal of Human Resources* 21: 485–506.

———, and Stephen G. Bronars. 1989. Consumer discrimination and self-employment. *Journal of Political Economy* 97: 581–605.

Bourdon, Clinton C., and Raymond E. Levitt. 1980. *Union and open-shop construction, compensation, work practices, and labor markets*. Lexington Books: Lexington, Mass.

Brimmer, Andrew F. 1966. The Negro in the national economy. In *American Negro reference book*, ed. John P. Davis, 251–336. Englewood Cliffs, N.J.: Prentice-Hall.

———. 1995. Economic growth and diversification of black-owned businesses. Paper presented in session, Studies of Minority-Owned Business. Annual Meeting of the National Economic Association. Washington, D.C.: Brimmer & Company, Inc., Economic Consultants.

———. 1997. Preamble: Blacks in the American economy: Summary of selected research. In *A different vision: African American economic thought, volume 1*, ed. Thomas D. Boston, 9–45. London: Routledge.

Brimmer, Andrew F., and Henry S. Terrell. 1971. The economic potential of black capitalism. *Public policy* 19(Spring):289–328.

Brimmer, Andrew F., and Ray Marshall. 1990. *Public policy and promotion of minority economic development: City of Atlanta and Fulton County, Georgia*. Washington, D.C.: Brimmer and Marshall Economic Consultants, Inc.

Brock, William A., David S. Evans, and Bruce D. Phillips. 1986. *The Economics of small businesses: their role and regulation in the U.S. economy*. New York: Holmes and Meier.

Bureau of the Census. *See* U.S. Bureau of the Census.

Cain, Glen G. 1986. The economic analysis of labor market discrimination: A survey. In *Handbook of labor economics, volume I*, ed. Orley Ashenfelter and Richard Layard, 693–785. Amsterdam: North-Holland.

California Legislature. 1996. Proposition 209, The California Civil Rights Initiative, a proposed statewide constitutional amendment by initiative.

Carson, Clayborne, David J. Garrow, Gerald Gill, Vincent Harding, and Darlene Clark Hine (eds.). 1991. *The eyes on the prize civil rights reader*. New York: Penguin Books.

Cayton, Horace R. and St. Clair Drake. 1946. *Black metropolis*. London: Jonathan Cape.

CIESIN. *See* Consortium for International Earth Science Information.

Cohen, David S. 1989. The evidentiary predicate for affirmative action after *Croson*: A proposal for shifting the burdens of proof. *Yale Law and Policy Review* 7:489–515.

Coles, Flournoy. 1969. *An analysis of black entrepreneurship in seven urban areas*. Washington, D.C.: The National Business League.

Connolly, Walter B., Jr., David W. Peterson, and Michael J. Connolly. 1996. *Use of statistics in equal employment opportunity litigation*. New York: Law Journal Seminars-Press.

Consortium for International Earth Science Information Network (CIESIN). 1996. MABLE/Geocorr database. Palisades, N.Y.

Cotton, Jeremiah. 1988. On the decomposition of wage differentials. *Review of Economics and Statistics* 70:236–43.

Council of State Community Development Agencies. 1993. *National directory of state minority business enterprise programs.* Washington, D.C.: Council of State Community Development Agencies.

Cross, Theodore L. 1971. A white paper on black capitalism. Boston: Gorham and Lamont, Inc.

Days, Drew S. 1990. Fullilove. In U.S. Congress, House, Committee on the Judiciary, *Minority business set-aside programs: The City of Richmond v. J. A. Croson Company: A collection of articles by constitutional scholars and economists,* 1–8. 101st Cong., 1st sess., January.

DeVine, Theresa J. 1994. Characteristics of self-employed women in the United States. *Monthly Labor Review* 117:20–34.

Ducat, Craig R. 1978. *Modes of constitutional interpretation.* St. Paul: West Publishing Company.

———, and Harold W. Chase. 1983. *Constitutional interpretation, 3rd ed.* St. Paul: West Publishing Company.

Duncan, Otis D. 1968. Inheritance of poverty or inheritance of race? In *On understanding poverty,* ed. D. P. Moynihan, 85–105. New York: Basic Books.

Dunlop, John. 1958. *Industrial relations systems.* New York: Henry Holt.

Eccles, Robert G. 1981. Bureaucratic versus Craft Administration: The Relationship of Market Structure to the Construction Firm. *Administrative Science Quarterly* 26.

Eltinge, John L., and William M. Sribney. 1996. Estimates of linear combinations and hypothesis tests for survey data. *Stata Technical Bulletin* 31: 31–42.

Enchautegui, Maria E., Michael Fix, Pamela Loprest, Sarah von der Lippe, and Douglas Wissoker. 1996. *Do minority-owned businesses get a fair share of government contracts?.* Washington, D.C.: The Urban Institute.

Evans, David S. 1998. Rebuttal report of defendant's expert. *Concrete Works of Colorado, Inc. v. The City and County of Denver.* United States District Court for the Southern District of Colorado. Civil Action No. 92 M 21. December.

———, and Boyan Jovanovic. 1989. An estimated model of entrepreneurial choice under liquidity constraints. *Journal of Political Economy* 97: 808–827.

———, and Linda S. Leighton. 1989. Some empirical aspects of entrepreneurship. *American Economic Review* 79:519–35.

Fairlie, Robert W. 1996. Ethnic and racial entrepreneurship: A study of historical and contemporary differences. New York and London: Garland Publishing, Inc.

Fairlee, Robert W., and Bruce D. Meyer. 1994. The ethnic and racial character of self-employment. *NBER Working Paper Series*. No. 4791.

———. 1996. Ethnic and racial self-employment differences and possible explanations. *Journal of Human Resources* 31:757–93.

Farmer, Richard T. 1968. Black businessmen in Indiana. *Indiana Business Review* 43 (November.).

Fitch, Daron S. 1992. The aftermath of *Croson*: A blueprint for a constitutionally permissible minority set-aside program. *Ohio State Law Journal* 53: 555–585.

Foley, Eugene. 1966. The Negro businessman: In search of a tradition. In *The Negro American*, eds. Talcott Parsons and Kenneth B. Clark. Boston: Houghton Mifflin.

Foster, M. J. "Mike", Jr., Governor of Louisiana. 1996. Executive Order MJF 96–1, January 11.

Fujii, Edwin T., and Clifford B. Hawley. 1991. Empirical aspects of self-employment. *Economics Letters* 36:323–29.

Frazier, E. Franklin. 1957. *The Negro in the United States, 2nd edition*. New York: Macmillan.

Gastwirth, Joseph L. 1988. *Statistical reasoning in law and public policy, volume 1: Statistical concepts and issues of fairness*. Boston: Academic Press, Inc.

General Services Commission. 1996. FY96 Statewide Historically Underutilized Business Report. Austin, Tex.: General Services Commission.

Ginzberg, Eli. 1956. *The Negro potential*. New York: Columbia University Press.

Goldberg, Matthew S. 1982. Discrimination, nepotism, and long-run wage differentials. *Quarterly Journal of Economics* 97 (2):307–19.

Goldstein, Barry. 1990. Set-asides after *City of Richmond v. J. A. Croson Company*. In U.S. Congress, House, Committee on the Judiciary, *Minority business set-aside programs: The City of Richmond v. J. A. Croson Company: A collection of articles by constitutional scholars and economists*, 35–42. 101st Cong., 1st sess., January.

Greene, William H. 1997. *Econometric analysis, 3rd edition*. Upper Saddle River, New Jersey: Prentice Hall.

Hamermesh, Daniel S. 1990. Data difficulties in labor economics, in *Fifty years of economic measurement*, eds. Ernst R. Berndt and Jack E. Triplett, 273–98. Chicago: University of Chicago Press.

Handy, John. 1989. *An analysis of black business enterprises*. New York and London: Garland Publishing, Inc.

Heckman, James J. and Guilherme L. Sedlacek. Self-selection and the distribution of hourly wages. *Journal of Labour Economics*. 8 (1, pt. 2):S329–S363.

Hills, George H. 1985. Black business and economics: A selected bibliography. New York and London: Garland Publishing, Inc.

Holtz-Eakin, Douglas, David Joulfaian, and Harvey S. Rosen. 1994. Entrepreneurial decisions and liquidity constraints. *RAND Journal of Economics* 25:334–47.

Hosmer, Jr., David W., and Stanley Lemeshow, 1989. *Applied logistic regression.* New York: John Wiley & Sons.

Johnson, Thomas. 1970. Returns from investment in human capital. *American Economic Review* 60:546–60.

Jones, Edward H. 1971. *Blacks in business.* New York: Grosset & Dunlap.

Kahn, Lawrence M. 1991. Customer discrimination and affirmative action. *Economic Inquiry* 29:555–571.

Kihlstrom, Richard E., and Jean-Jacques Laffont. 1979. A general equilibrium entrepreneurial theory of firm formation based on risk aversion. *Journal of Political Economy.* 87. 719–748.

Killingsworth, Mark R. and James J. Heckman. 1986. Female labor supply: A survey. In *Handbook of labor economics, volume 1*, eds. Orley Ashenfelter and Richard Layard, 103–204. Amsterdam: North-Holland.

King, Martin Luther, Jr. 1963. Letter from Birmingham city jail (April 16). In *The eyes on the prize civil rights reader*, eds. Carson, *et al.*, 153–58. New York: Penguin Books.

Kish, Leslie. 1965. *Survey Sampling.* New York: John Wiley & Sons, Inc.

Kitigawa, Evelyn M. 1955. Components of a difference between two rates. *Journal of the American Statistical Association.* 50:1168–1194.

Knight, Frank H. [1921] 1965. *Risk, uncertainty, and profit.* New York: Harper and Row.

La Noue, George R. 1994a. Local officials guide: Minority business programs and disparity studies. Washington, DC: National League of Cities

———. 1994b. Standards for the second generation of *Croson*-inspired disparity studies. *The Urban Lawyer* 26:485–540.

Lazear, Edward P. 1986. Retirement from the labor force. In *Handbook of labor economics, volume 1*, ed. Orley Ashenfelter and Richard Layard, 305–356. Amsterdam: North-Holland.

Lucas, Robert E. 1978. On the size distribution of business firms. *Bell Journal of Economics.* 9. 508–23.

Lunn, John, and Huey L. Perry. 1993. Justifying affirmative action: Highway construction in Louisiana. *Industrial and Labor Relations Review.* 46. 464–479.

McCloskey, Dierdre N., and Stephen T. Ziliak. 1996. The standard error of regressions. *Journal of Economic Literature* 34:91–114.

Maddala, G.S. 1983. *Limited dependent and qualitative variables in econometrics*. Cambridge: Cambridge University Press.

Malkiel, Burton G. And Judith A. Malkiel. 1973. Male-female pay differentials in professional employment. *American Economic Review* 63:693–705.

Marshall, Ray. 1965. *The Negro and organized labor*. New York: John Wiley and Sons.

———. 1967. *The Negro worker*. New York: Random House.

———. 1974. The economics of racial discrimination. *Journal of Economic Literature* 12:849–871.

———. 1991a. Civil rights and social equity: Beyond Neoclassical theory. In *New directions in civil rights studies*, eds. Armstead L. Robinson and Patricia Sullivan, 149–74. Charlottesville: Univ. Press of Virginia.

———. 1991b. Minority and female business development after *Croson*. Unpublished manuscript.

———, and Vernon M. Briggs, Jr. 1989. *Labor economics: Theory, institutions, and public policy*. Homewood, Ill: Irwin.

———, and Virgil L. Christian, Jr. 1978. Economics of employment discrimination. In *Employment of blacks in the south: A perspective on the 1960s*, eds. Ray Marshall and Virgil L. Christian, Jr., 205–36. Austin: University of Texas Press.

MBELDEF. *See* Minority Business Enterprise Legal Defense and Education Fund, Inc.

Meier, Paul, Jerome Sacks, and Sandy L. Zabell. 1986. What happened in Hazelwood: Statistics, employment discrimination, and the 80% rule. In *Statistics and the law*. DeGroot, Morris H., Stephen E. Fienberg, and Joseph B. Kadane (eds.), 1–40. New York: John Wiley & Sons.

Meyer, Bruce D. 1990. Why are there so few black entrepreneurs? *NBER Working Paper Series*. Working paper no. 3537.

Mincer, Jacob. 1970. The distribution of labor incomes: A survey with special reference to the human capital approach. *Journal of Economic Literature* 8(March):1–26.

Minority Business Enterprise Legal Defense and Education Fund, Inc. 1988. *Report on the minority business enterprise programs of state and local governments*. Washington, DC: MBELDEF, Inc.

———. 1991. *The effect of "Croson" and similar attacks on federal, state, and local MBE, WBE, and DBE programs nationwide*. Washington, DC: MBELDEF, Inc.

Moore, Robert L. 1983. Employer discrimination: Evidence from self-employed workers. *The Review of Economics and Statistics* 65:496–501.

Myrdal, Gunnar. [1944] 1962. *An American dilemma*. New York: Harper and Row.

National Economic Research Associates, Inc. 1994. *The State of Texas disparity study*. Austin, Tex.: Comptroller of Public Accounts.

NERA. *See* National Economic Research Associates, Inc.

Neuman, Shoshana and Jacques Silber. 1994. The econometrics of labor market segregation and discrimination. *Journal of Econometrics* 61:1–4.

Neumark, David. 1988. Employers' discriminatory behavior and the estimation of wage discrimination. *Journal of Human Resources* 23:279–95.

Northrup, Herbert R. [1944] 1971. Organized labor and the Negro. New York: Harper. Reprinted, New York: Kraus Reprint Co.

Oaxaca, Ronald L. 1973. Male-female wage differentials in urban labor markets. *International Economic Review* 9:693–709.

———, and Michael R. Ransom. 1994. On discrimination and the decomposition of wage differentials. *Journal of Econometrics* 61:5–21.

Payton, John. 1990. The meaning and significance of the *Croson* case. In U.S. Congress, House, Committee on the Judiciary, *Minority business set-aside programs: The City of Richmond v. J. A. Croson Company: A collection of articles by constitutional scholars and economists*, 13–34. 101st Cong., 1st sess., January.

Pencavel, John. Labor supply of men: A survey. In *Handbook of labor economics, volume 1*, ed. Orley Ashenfelter and Richard Layard, 3–102. Amsterdam: North-Holland.

Pierce, Joseph. 1947. *Negro business and business education*. New York: Harper Brothers.

Riemers, Cordelia. 1984. Labor market discrimination against Hispanic and black men. *Review of Economics and Statistics* 65:570–79.

Rigelhaupt, James L. 1976. Racial discrimination in employment (in general; use of statistics). *American Jurisprudence: Proof of Facts* 2d ser., no. 2:187–235.

Rosen, Sherwin. 1986. The theory of equalizing differences. In *Handbook of labor economics, volume 1*, ed. Orley Ashenfelter and Richard Layard, 641–92. Amsterdam: North-Holland.

Sattinger, Michael. 1993. Assignment models in the distribution of earnings. *Journal of Economic Literature*. 31:831–880.

Schumpeter, Joseph Alois. [1912] 1961. *The theory of economic development*. Leipzig: Duncker & Humblot. Trans. R. Opie, Cambridge, Mass.: Harvard University Press. Reprinted, New York: Oxford University Press.

Silvestri, George T. 1991. Who are the self-employed? Employment profiles and recent trends. *Occupational Outlook Quarterly* 35:26–36.

Snipp, C. Matthew. 1989. *American Indians: The first of this land*. New York: Russell Sage Foundation.

Stafford, Frank. 1986. Forestalling the demise of empirical economics: The role of microdata in labor economics research. In *Handbook of labor economics, volume I*, ed. Orley Ashenfelter and Richard Layard, 387–428. Amsterdam: North-Holland.

Stephanopoulos, George, and Christopher Edley, Jr. 1995. *Affirmative action review report to the president*. Washington, D.C.: The White House.

Suggs, Robert E. 1990. Making equal opportunity pay. In U.S. Congress, House, Committee on the Judiciary, *Minority business set-aside programs: The City of Richmond v. J. A. Croson Company: A collection of articles by constitutional scholars and economists*, 89–92. 101st Cong., 1st sess., January.

Thompson, Steven K. 1992. *Sampling*. New York: John Wiley & Sons.

Thurow, Lester C. 1969. *Poverty and discrimination*. Washington, D.C.: The Brookings Institution.

U.S. Bureau of the Census. 1990. *1987 economic censuses: Women-owned businesses*. Washington, D.C.: The Census Bureau.

———. 1991a. *1987 economic censuses: Survey of minority-owned business enterprises: Black*. Washington, D.C.: The Census Bureau.

———. 1991b. *1987 economic censuses: Survey of minority-owned business enterprises: Hispanic*. Washington, D.C.: The Census Bureau.

———. 1991c. *1987 economic censuses: Survey of minority-owned business enterprises: Asian Americans, American Indians, and Other Minorities*. Washington, D.C.: The Census Bureau.

———. 1991d. *1987 economic censuses: Survey of minority-owned business enterprises: Summary*. Washington, D.C.: The Census Bureau.

———. 1991e. *1987 economic censuses: Characteristics of Business Owners*. Washington, D.C.: The Census Bureau.

———. 1991f. *1987 economic censuses: Survey of minority-owned business enterprises: Table 4. Statistics for All U.S. Firms by Industry Division for Metropolitan Statistical Areas*. Photocopy [unpublished].

———. 1991g. *Current population survey, March 1988–1991 on CD-ROM technical documentation*. Washington, D.C.: The Census Bureau.

———. 1991h. *State and metropolitan area data book 1991, 4th edition*. Washington, DC: The Bureau.

———. 1991i. *Statistical abstract of the United States: 1991*. Washington, D.C.: The Census Bureau.

———. 1992a. *Census of population and housing, 1990: Public use microdata samples U.S. technical documentation*. Washington, D.C.: The Census Bureau.

———. 1992b. *Statistical Abstract of the United States: 1992*. Washington, D.C.: The Census Bureau.

———. 1993. *Census of population and housing, 1990: Public use microdata samples U.S.* [machine-readable data files]. Washington, D.C.: The Census Bureau.

————. 1996a. *1992 economic censuses: Survey of minority-owned business enterprises: Black.* Washington, D.C.: The Census Bureau.

————. 1996b. *1992 economic censuses: Survey of minority-owned business enterprises: Hispanic.* Washington, D.C.: The Census Bureau.

————. 1996c. *1992 economic censuses: Survey of minority-owned business enterprises: Asian Americans, American Indians, and Other Minorities.* Washington, D.C.: The Census Bureau.

————. 1996d. *1992 economic censuses: Survey of minority-owned business enterprises: Summary.* Washington, D.C.: The Census Bureau.

————. 1996e. *1992 economic censuses: Survey of minority-owned business enterprises: Table 1u.* Photocopy [unpublished].

————. 1996f. *1992 economic censuses: Survey of minority-owned business enterprises: Table 2. Statistics for All U.S. Firms by Industry Division for Metropolitan Areas: 1992.* Photocopy [unpublished].

U.S. Congress, House. 1995. *A Bill To Prohibit Discrimination and Preferential Treatment on the Basis of Race, Color, National Origin, or Sex with Respect to Federal Employment, Contracts, and Programs.* 104th Cong., 1st sess., H.R. 2128.

U.S. Congress, Senate. 1995 *A Bill To Prohibit Discrimination and Preferential Treatment on the Basis of Race, Color, National Origin, or Sex with Respect to Federal Employment, Contracts, and Programs.* 104th Cong., 1st sess., S. 1085.

U.S. Small Business Administration. 1996. *The state of small business: A report of the president.* Washington, D.C.: Government Printing Office.

VanMiddlesworth, Rex D. 1995. What's next for affirmative action? *Texas Lawyer* (June 26): 26–28.

Wainwright, Jon. 1991. Racial discrimination in the construction industry: Measurement of disparities. In *Racial discrimination and disparities in the market place: Metropolitan Dade County, Florida*, ed. Andrew Brimmer, Part III. Washington, D.C.: Brimmer & Company, Inc.

Washington, Booker T. 1907. *The Negro in business.* Boston: Hertel, Jenkins & Co.

Weiss, Yoram. 1986. The determination of life-cycle earnings: A survey. In *Handbook of labor economics, volume 1*, ed. Orley Ashenfelter and Richard Layard, 603–640. Amsterdam: North-Holland.

Welch, Finis. 1967. Labor market discrimination: An interpretation of income differences in the rural South. *Journal of Political Economy* 65:225–40.

Willis, Robert J. 1986. Wage determinants: A survey and reinterpretation of human capital earnings functions. In *Handbook of labor economics, volume 1*, ed. Orley Ashenfelter and Richard Layard, 525–602. Amsterdam: North-Holland.

Wilson, Peter. J. "Pete". 1995. Executive order abolishing affirmative action in state university admissions (June 1).

Index

Page numbers followed by *t* indicate tables.